the family

the family

BY ROBERT WERNICK

AND THE EDITORS OF TIME-LIFE BOOKS

TIME-LIFE BOOKS, NEW YORK

The Author: Robert Wernick is a Paris-based freelance writer who was formerly on the staff of *Life.* He is the author of *The Monument Builders* for TIME-LIFE BOOKS and of four other volumes, one a novel about family life in the 1930s. He has also written on psychology, art and other subjects.

General Consultants for Human Behavior: Robert M. Krauss is Professor of Psychology at Columbia University. He has taught at Princeton and Harvard and was Chairman of the Psychology Department at Rutgers. He is the co-author of *Theories in Social Psychology,* edits the *Journal of Experimental Social Psychology,* and contributes articles to many journals on aspects of human behavior and social interaction.

Peter I. Rose, a specialist on racial and ethnic relations, is Chairman of the Department of Sociology and Anthropology at Smith College and is on the graduate faculty of the University of Massachusetts. His books include *The Subject Is Race, The Ghetto and Beyond* and *Americans from Africa.* Professor Rose has also taught at Goucher, Wesleyan, Colorado, Clark, Yale, Amherst, the University of Leicester in England, Kyoto University in Japan and Flinders University in Australia.

James W. Fernandez is Chairman of the Anthropology Department at Dartmouth College. His research in culture change has taken him to East, West and South Africa and the Iberian peninsula. Articles on his field studies have been widely published in European and American anthropology journals. He has been president of the Northeastern Anthropological Association and a consultant to the Foreign Service Institute.

Special Consultant for The Family: Hyman Rodman, Senior Research Associate at the Merrill-Palmer Institute of Human Development and Family Life in Detroit, Michigan, is co-author of *The Abortion Controversy* and author of *Lower Class Families: The Culture of Poverty in Negro Trinidad; Marriage, Family and Society;* and *Teaching About Families.* He served as consultant to the National Advisory Commission on Civil Disorder and is a former editor of *Social Problems.*

Valuable assistance was given by the following departments and individuals of Time Inc.: Editorial Production, Norman Airey; Library, Benjamin Lightman; Picture Collection, Doris O'Neil; Photographic Laboratory, George Karas; TIME-LIFE News Service, Murray J. Gart; Correspondents Ann Natanson (Rome), Margot Hapgood and Dorothy Bacon (London), Maria Vincenza Aloisi and Josephine du Brusle (Paris), Elisabeth Kraemer (Bonn), Lucretia Marmon and William Marmon (Jerusalem), S. Chang and Frank Iwama (Tokyo), Peter Hawthorne (Johannesburg), James Shepherd (New Delhi), Bing Wong (Hong Kong), Ruth Galvin (Boston), Bernard Diederich (Mexico City).

Contents

The Eternal Family

1

Human history, according to Judeo-Christian theology, began with a family in crisis: the marital discord of Adam and Eve, the sibling rivalry of Cain and Abel. In the mythology of the classical Greeks, the principal crisis was the revolt of Zeus and his brothers against the tyrannical rule of their father Cronus, while in legends of North Australia's Stone-age Wulamba, the crucial episode was the theft of tribal secrets by brothers from their sisters. In modern times, Freud has described the primal human event as the banding together of brothers in a savage horde whose members killed and ate their father in order to possess their mother.

At the base of all these disparate systems of thought, there is a sense of the family as something primordial, essential to the existence of man, and at the same time a sense of instability, conflict and change and crisis.

The crisis can indeed be called eternal. There has probably never been a generation from Adam's to the present that did not, in some way, feel certain that the family as an institution was breaking down and that the good old customs were being drowned in laxity and in permissiveness. It is very easy to understand why. People form their idea of what a family should be when they are very young and impressionable. By the time they have grown up, the world has changed, and the family, that most adaptable of human institutions, has changed with it; things are no longer the way they were in grandpa's day.

The world changes at different rates at different times. Most people think of the present century as the one that has most radically changed the human condition. It is debatable whether other centuries have not seen changes just as drastic, but it is beyond dispute that change these days is more nearly universal than ever before: all corners of the globe are caught up in the process. Industrialization, urbanization, the deification of the nation-state, the breakdown of traditional religious and moral codes, the spread of secularism, the consumer-oriented economy—everything combines to put old family structures under strain on a global scale. Relationships basic to family life—between young and old, between men and women—are undergoing transformation. The African chief sees his sons go off to work in a new city and set up housekeeping with girls from other tribes who do not speak the ancestral language and who will bring up their children unaware of ancestral gods and customs. The elderly Japanese gentleman chokes as he sees women sitting down at the same table with their husbands and even getting into the bath ahead of them. The aging immigrant in America sees his grandchildren choosing wives and husbands without consulting their elders, much less letting them make the preliminary negotiations. It is only natural for older generations to conclude that the family is sick unto death.

Statistics are hardly reassuring. In the early 1970s, one marriage of every three in the United States ended in divorce. In West Germany, the ratio was one out of seven; in the Soviet Union, one out of four; in Japan, one out of 10. Runaways were a multiplying breed. Every year as many as 100,000 American husbands fled the pressures of home and family to begin a new and secret life. Although no totals were available for women, one New York private detective reported that in 1973 nearly 50 per cent of the absent spouses he tried to trace were women. In 1969, he said, the figure had been only 2 per cent. In another form of revolt against the family, thousands of young men and women opted to live in communes, where they worked, played and raised children outside traditional family organization and traditional patterns of male-female relationships.

Indeed, it was the revolution in relations between the sexes that most dismayed family traditionalists. The centuries-old conviction that women's place was in the home weakened both in the underdeveloped villages of Asia and Africa and in the sophisticated cities of Europe and America, as female workers filled factories and offices. In the Soviet Union 75 per cent of the physicians were women. In the United States, more than half of all wives held paying jobs. And as wives worked, many husbands took on some household and child-care duties.

But even a fundamental change in an ancient division of labor was not so unsettling as new attitudes toward sexual relations. Through most of the Western world men and women were taking a more casual view of sex, in and out of marriage. A 1972 study by Johns Hopkins demographers Melvin Zelnik and John Kantner suggested that nearly half of all single American girls were engaging in sexual intercourse before they were 20. Other studies pointed to a like situation in Scandinavia, West Germany and elsewhere in the Western world. Increasingly often, experimentation led to "arrangements" between young unmarried couples who lived together openly. In one rural town, a nursery-school teacher lived with a local construction worker without rousing public stir. At Harvard Medical School, women students discussed not only where they were going to practice but whether they would marry or just live with someone. In many countries, women were deciding that they did not want to marry at all, and single motherhood was becoming a middle-class phenomenon in the United States, Canada and Western Europe. In Montreal, for example, up to 55 per cent of the unmarried women who bore babies in 1973 decided to bring up their infants alone, compared to only 20 per cent in 1967.

Such is the evidence leading many preachers, politicians and social scientists to take it as an article of faith that the modern family is hopelessly in trouble. Not long ago, one behavioral expert alleged that "the family has lost its power and direction"; another warned that the family "is in for a severe upheaval"; and a third branded the family as "a fur-lined bear trap" that drives some of its members into madness. Less given to vivid imagery, some anthropologists, sociologists and psychiatrists have nonetheless written ominously of "the decline of the family," or of its "disintegration," "decay," "collapse"—and even of its "death."

All these Jeremiahs may be right. Yet the family is the oldest and toughest of all human institutions; it has already outlasted much that seemed eternal: gods, empires, systems of political economy. If families are not what they used to be, it may be that they are not disappearing but changing. What is for one observer a loss of essential ingredients may be for another an alteration of form and function. Thus a hard look at the family must begin with some agreement on what a family is. The word in ordinary discourse is markedly ambiguous: when a person speaks of his family, he may be referring to his immediate household, or to a whole network of grandparents and second cousins, or even to a whole stretch of generations going back hundreds of years. Thus all generalizations about the family are dangerous. One way to begin shaping a definition is to prune away attributes that are found in some families but not in all.

It is commonly assumed that the family is based on a hereditary bond between parents and the children they bear, and so, generally, it is. But almost all societies provide some means for adopting children, who may come of entirely different stock from the foster parents and yet be regarded as their descendants and heirs. Obviously, then, a biological tie is not an essential family ingredient.

Most families follow a rule of common residence for parents and children. But by no means all. Among some people in New Guinea, reports anthropologist Ruth Benedict, the mother lives apart from her husband, who visits her surreptitiously at home or in the bush. The children are brought up under the supervision of their mother's family, and while they know perfectly well who their father is, they rarely see him. In other cultures, the husband may be away most of the time if he is a sailor or a traveling salesman; the children may be off at boarding schools; and in former centuries they might have been cared for by nurses from the day of their birth.

In the past, the family made up an economic unit that came close to being self-sufficient. On the farms where most people lived until a couple of generations ago, parents and children worked together at their respective tasks to keep themselves supplied with the necessities of life. But in the modern industrial world, the family no longer subsists on homemade food, clothes and tools. Husband, wife and teen-age children may all hold separate jobs, and while the parents nearly always pool part of their earnings, the family no longer comprises a tight economic entity, a closely bound unit of production and consumption.

It is generally assumed that families perform what social scientists call

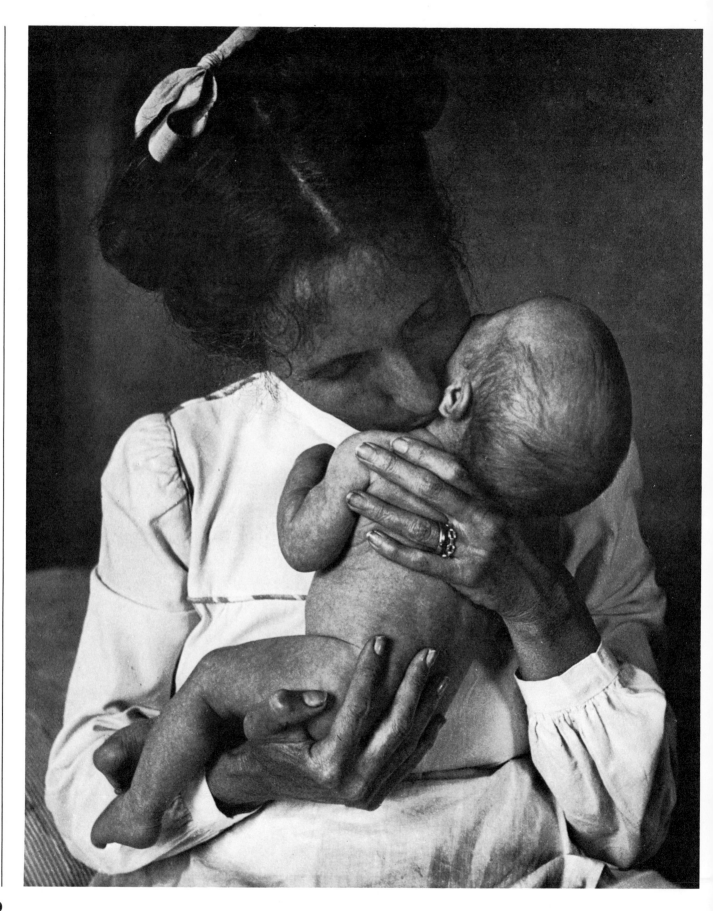

an affectional function, serving at best as a source of love and providing at least a sense of belonging to something. True enough, a typical family forms a compact unit in which each of its members finds some comfort and protection from the dangers of the unknown outside. It develops its own defenses, its own quirks and peculiarities that mark its members off from other people, and these all help bind it together emotionally in a kind of cozy conspiracy. A family often has its private jokes, its private rituals, its private myths that only its members can share. A majority of people form the deepest and most lasting of their emotional involvements with members of their families, and it is to the family that they are most likely to turn when disaster strikes. "Home," said Robert Frost, "is the place where, when you go there, they have to take you in." Or as a southern migrant worker told a sociologist, it is "a place to go back to if things get rough out here."

Yet some cultures do not consider love between husband and wife an essential element in the family relationship. Even in Western cultures, where marriage for love is the ideal, everyone knows that there is more hate than affection between some husbands and wives. Some experts have estimated that no more than 25 per cent of American marriages are emotionally satisfying, and sociologists have described "empty shell families," in which the members go on living together even though there is little emotional interaction or, indeed, communication of any kind between them. They are still families, but the affectional function is lacking.

Some families have filled, and continue to fill, still other functions. These may be religious, as in ancient Rome where the father in every household was a kind of priest, responsible for perpetuating the worship of the household gods. In parts of the Orient to this day, the life of the family is organized around the cult of the ancestors who founded the line in a far-off past. But such religious functions are in decline almost everywhere. In the average Western family there remain only vestigial rites like saying grace before meals or setting up a Christmas tree. Evidently, the family can survive without being a religious unit.

It need not carry out political functions either, although in many parts of the world it does that. In feudal societies, families may pass down honors and positions of state along with the heirlooms. In England, great families of landed gentry have included members holding high office generation after generation: William Cecil was Lord Treasurer and chief advisor to Queen Elizabeth I, and his great-great-great-great-great-great-great-great-great-grandson, Robert Cecil, was Parliamentary Under Secretary of State for Foreign Affairs and Leader of the House of Lords during the reign of Queen Elizabeth II. Even in the United States, one of the most individualistic of all societies, bloc voting by families is familiar to politicians. But everywhere in the modern world, husbands and wives, parents and children, can form a harmonious family without belonging to the same political party and even without participating in politics at all.

What is left after all these attributes of some families have been found not essential to all? Only this: a family is a small group of people who consider themselves bound by enduring ties and who accept the responsibility for bringing up children. For the children the family performs two crucial functions. First, it cares for them physically so that they will not die and so that they will grow up healthy and strong. Second, it transforms them from mere biological organisms into human beings who can function as members of the society into which they were born.

The first of these functions is readily comprehensible and rests on a solid biological basis. When the human infant is born, he is not physically equipped to survive on his own, and he remains immature and dependent for a longer time than the young of any other animal. He cannot work productively till the age of six or so, and most societies do not consider him fit for full adult responsibilities until at least the onset of puberty, sometimes not until much later. Until ready for those responsibilities, the child needs older people to take care of him.

The simplest and most logical choice for care of the infant is his parents. Presumably, for the first human families wandering the Pleistocene forests and savannahs, there was little choice. A child had to be fed by his mother or he would die, and she in turn had to be given sustenance and protection by a man while she was tied down bearing and feeding children. This man was likely to be the physical father of her offspring. The reason is linked by many scientists to human biology. There is no oestrus or special period of sexual excitability in Homo sapiens as there is in most animals, and thus the female as well as the male is always sexually available. This continuing sexual relationship fosters a more or less lasting attachment between a man and a woman; a man more often than not goes on living with his woman and their children long after the moment of conception. This pattern is not universal, however, and the father and mother in a family can be any man and woman to whom society grants the parental roles. What is universal are the roles themselves. A child may be brought up by any mother and any father, not necessarily his biological parents, so long as they regard him as part of the family, offering him the physical and emotional care that will enable him to develop as a member of the society of which they form a part.

The second family function, the making of a true human being from what is, to begin with, not much more than a cuddly blob of flesh, is much more complex. Behavioral scientists call the metamorphosis socialization or enculturation. Both words are fancy terms for the processes of indoctrination and teaching by which the patterns of human behavior are transmitted from one generation to the next. Without socialization, cultures would die and people would be animals.

History is full of stories of "wolf children," abandoned youngsters raised by wild animals whom they come to resemble. None of these tales has been adequately authenticated, but it does not really matter whether they are fact or myth. The point they make is undeniably true. It has been proved beyond question by recent, well-documented cases of "attic children": unwanted, often illegitimate babies kept hidden by their mothers in places where they are periodically fed and washed but infrequently fondled or spoken to. One such case has been described by sociologist Kingsley Davis. In 1938, a social worker discovered a little girl tied to a chair in an attic-like room on her grandfather's Pennsylvania farm. Anna had been confined there by her mother during most of her short life because her grandfather resented her illegitimacy and did not want to be reminded of her existence. Although nearly six years old when found, she did not talk, smile, cry or respond in any other way to people around her. When she was moved to a foster home, she eventually became less apathetic, but she remained socially and mentally retarded and never learned to speak more than a few sentences. Her case was not atypical; unless children like Anna are rescued very early, they never master language or respond normally. Lacking families to bring them up, they have not been socialized, they are not part of a society and thus in a real sense they are not human.

The key to humanization is language, the gift that distinguishes man from the rest of the animal kingdom. Its importance becomes clear not only in the experience of the attic children but also in the case of deaf children, who tend to be socially and intellectually backward until they learn to use words. Witness the case of Helen Keller, the noted author who lost both sight and hearing as an infant: Her world was transformed when, at the age of almost seven years, one of her hands was held under a pump as her teacher Annie Sullivan spelled the word water into the other. "Somehow," Keller wrote years later, "the mystery of language was revealed to me. . . . I knew then that 'w-a-t-e-r' meant the wonderful cool something that was flowing over my hand. That living word awakened my soul, gave it light, hope, joy, set it free! Everything had a name, and each name gave birth to a new thought."

The characteristic tenor of any human being's thoughts depends partly on what language he learns from his parents. The child whose family speaks English is going to connect with the world in somewhat different ways from the child whose family speaks French. This is true even though, from the point of view of the linguist, French and English are related languages, coming from the same Indo-European stock, with differing vocabularies but much the same sentence structure and grammatical logic. There are other language stocks that have totally different structures and outlooks. For instance, the child brought up learning a language like Hopi, which does not differentiate between past, present and future in its verbs, will have a different conception of time, and as a result a very different outlook on life and on the world, from the offspring of the French- or English-speaking family. In a similar way, language will influence all parts of the socialization process simply because, after babyhood, language is the medium of most learning.

To convert the raw material of a child into a civilized human being, the child's family must convey to him a heritage made up of three parts: knowl-

Culture by example

All parents are models. They have to be if they are to fulfill their basic family obligation of preparing their children for adult life. The children learn to speak by listening to their parents and talking with them; they acquire their moral values and standards of conduct by observing their parents; and they learn their sex roles and how to survive in their own particular cultures in the same way.

In the initial stages, the child may imitate either parent indiscriminately (above). Later, by noting whether the parent's response is approving, the child quickly discovers which behavior and which role is appropriate for him.

Mimicking her father, a three-year-old practices the motions of shaving, a skill she will never have to master, but one that helps her understand sex roles.

A Navajo girl in Arizona watches her mother weave. By the time she is 12 or 13, she will learn enough of the art to join the ranks of village weavers.

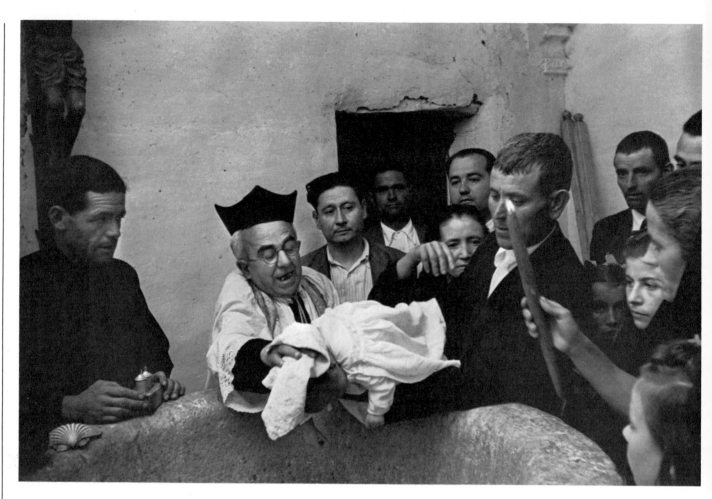

edge, patterns of social behavior and values. In the first place, the child must be taught some basic facts and skills so that he can survive in his world. Second, he must be trained in habits of acting that enable him to get along with the people he lives with. And third, he must be indoctrinated with his family's values—their assessment of what is important and what is not—so that his actions can be directed toward the goals peculiar to his subunit of society. These three elements of socialization are intricately intermixed; each heavily influences the others—values, for example, determining what knowledge is learned and what patterns of behavior are adopted. The nature of the elements obviously varies widely from culture to culture—what is known or prized or done could hardly be the same in a Chinese fishing village as in Paris. But surprisingly, great variation in socialization also occurs within families of the same culture.

To parents in preliterate societies, it is vital that their offspring learn which plants and berries are edible and which poisonous, which animals may attack and which can safely be approached and captured for food. In modern technological societies, children often remain ignorant of nature even though they may devote years of study to chemistry, physics and mathematics. When it comes to skills, or patterns of physical behavior, there is the same cultural variation. Youthful Eskimos are taught fishing techniques, for instance, while Japanese peasants learn how to grow rice. Young Americans learn to drive cars in their teens if not before, young Norwegians often master skiing before they turn five, and Manus children in New Guinea learn to swim about as soon as they can toddle. As Margaret Mead has reported of the Manus, "There is not a child of five who can't swim well. A Manus child who couldn't swim would be as aberrant, as definitely subnormal, as an American child of five who couldn't walk."

Subtler, perhaps, are the family variations in facts and skills taught to children. For each family exerts its own influence on the balance of knowledge that will be learned by its younger members. Nearly all children in the Western nations, for example, are encouraged and if necessary forced by their parents to learn the basic skill of civilization, reading. But there is wide variation in the degree of skill attained and the amount of use the skill gets. These differences cannot be ascribed entirely to individual aptitudes or even to subcultural pressures, such as the ethnic and economic factors that affect the value placed by parents on reading skills. Such influences aside, the fact remains that some parents create a climate that encourages reading—they keep many kinds of books and magazines readily available, they read to their children regularly, they help teach reading, they constantly discuss subjects that are read about. In those families, children learn to read earlier, they attain better and easier comprehension of printed material, they enjoy reading more and they read more than their peers. Reading has been made one of the most important aspects of their socialization, and for that reason it becomes one of the most important parts of their adult lives.

The family influence is equally noticeable in the second category of the socialization process, that directed toward the development of patterns of social behavior. The family provides the child his first lessons in getting along with other people. The first time he has to wait for feeding, a baby begins to learn that he must sometimes adjust his appetites and actions to the needs and demands of others. Eventually he comes to understand that he does well to follow certain formulas in expressing his own needs. He learns that he may have to moderate his protests when the world is slow to meet his demands, and that "please" and "may I?" often make it easier to get what is wanted. Yet he may also learn when—and with whom—blunt insistence or a display of violence is more effective than moderation and patience. As the child grows older he finds out how, as well as under what circumstances, he can legitimately call for help, when he is expected to give it to others and what ways of helping are considered most appropriate.

Other patterns learned in the course of socialization have to do with status, or social position. Within a given society, the family makes sure that the child learns early to what class or rank or station in life he is born, exactly what his society expects of someone occupying his particular niche, and also what kinds of behavior will be rewarded, punished or simply ignored. The simple admonition "Nice girls don't do that" carries with it many overtones of meaning to the girl addressed: her action is forbidden,

in this place and time, to a female of her age and her family. At a different age or in different circumstances, it might be permissible. Children are taught manners, modes of dress and preferences in recreation that suit their class, and even more important, the attitudes that fit their station.

Even if their station is intolerable, those who refuse to be bound by this part of the socialization process run grave risks. The results can, in extreme cases, be tragic. As recently as 1955, a young black named Emmett Till was brutally murdered by whites on a visit to a small town in the U.S. South because he did not "know his place." Raised in a northern city where color lines were less rigid, he was not aware of patterns of behavior then enforced in the rural South, and he breached them by whistling at a white woman. For this action he was killed.

The rules of status are so important because they depend heavily on values, the third category of cultural material handed down in the family during the socialization process. Values are simply attitudes: standards by which people measure the relative worth of everything from material objects to philosophical ideas, from personality characteristics to life goals and ways of achieving them. Through socialization every human being learns what his society—and his family—respects or disdains, loves or hates, idealizes or scorns.

One of the subtlest expressions of a family-induced value that influences social behavior was observed by Jerome Bruner, the distinguished Oxford psychologist. He concluded from studies on the subject that one reliable indicator of a child's social class in modern society is how he answers the question, "What do you think is more important in determining success, ability or luck?" Most lower-class children, whose economically deprived parents have little reason to anticipate success by their own exertions, answer "luck." Middle-class youngsters, who have been brought up to believe that effort brings its just reward—and who have observed that in their social class it does exactly that—usually reply "ability." These class convictions, handed down from parent to child, have a profound effect on patterns of social behavior. Children of poverty are likely to develop poor work habits at school, not because they are lazy or stupid but because they expect to gain nothing from hard work. Middle-class boys and girls, believing that ability pays off, are more likely to come to school with their homework done, listen attentively when teachers are speaking, shun disruptive behavior and use colored pens for underlining important passages in schoolbooks rather than for writing on walls.

Such distinctions in values and behavior between classes in a culture are overshadowed by the differences between cultures. Willa Cather has pointed out that the American Indian is raised to feel a sense of identification with nature; he moves across the landscape in such a way as to leave the least possible trace of his passage. The white American child, on the other hand, learns early that nature is something to be struggled with, and that making a mark in the world is one of the highest goals in life.

While cooperation with nature was prized by nearly all Indians, their attitudes toward fellow humans varied. Some, like the Sioux and Comanche, were intensely competitive. Others shunned competition; the Hopi are so reluctant to win over one another that they cannot be given ordinary tests—no one will attempt to provide correct answers lest he outshine his companions. The Russians value a similar submersion of individual glory. Their society encourages rivalry not between individuals but among social groups; within each group, members are expected to cooperate rather than compete with one another toward a common end. When psychologist Urie Bronfenbrenner visited Soviet classrooms, he saw charts on display that asked, "Who's Best?" and then cited not one child but a row of youngsters. When an individual was praised, it was most often because he had helped his group. "Today Pyotor helped Katya," one teacher said, "and as a result his unit did not get behind the rest."

The goals of the socialization process vary from society to society and family to family—each group differing from others in the knowledge, behavior patterns and values it will inculcate in its children—but the importance of the process does not vary. Converting the infant anarchist into a useful member of a group is, after physical survival, the essential function of every family everywhere. And every family everywhere employs the same basic methods in socializing the child. Though emphases and details may differ, all families communicate the cultural curriculum —and make it stick—in three ways: by prohibition or command, by example, and through reward and punishment. Sometimes the teaching is direct and explicit. More often it is subtle and even unconscious, the parent teaching without even intending to teach and the child absorbing the lesson without knowing that he is learning.

In American families the dos and don'ts are likely to be explicit and frequent. They are so much a part of the child's experience that he may use them to help along the socialization process. Psychoanalyst Selma Fraiberg explains how a child may "incorporate" verbal prohibitions, making them part of himself to control the impulses his family finds offensive. Incorporation takes time to become effective, however, as Fraiberg illustrates with a charming story about Julia, a girl of 30 months irresistibly tempted by a bowl of eggs. As Fraiberg tells it, "When Julia's mother returns to the kitchen, she finds her daughter cheerfully plopping eggs on the linoleum and scolding herself sharply for each plop, 'NoNoNo. Musn't dood it. NoNoNo. *Musn't* dood it!' "

More delicate than don't or mustn't, and much more effective as a technique of socialization, is example. Inadvertently, mothers and fathers convey a great deal to their offspring just by performing their habitual tasks, enjoying their usual pleasures and living their customary lives. Children are great imitators: they are likely to copy a parent's way of setting a table, driving a golf ball—or making out a false income-tax return. In most cultures, teaching by example is also undertaken intentionally, often through entertaining stories that point a moral or glorify a way of life. The Indians of the North American Great Plains hoped that their boys

So strong are family ties that attempts are made to preserve them even after death, as is poignantly illustrated by this 1799 Vermont gravestone depicting a mother buried between her children.

would become heroic fighters, and so they tried to inspire them by recounting tales of great warriors worthy of emulation.

To buttress their teachings, all families rely on reward or punishment or both. In many cultures, reward may mean a smile, a hug, an affectionate word; punishment, a frown, a spank, a sharp reproof. American parents frequently reinforce good behavior with material gifts such as money or a transistor radio or a TV set for a youngster's bedroom. A favorite punishment is withdrawal of privileges—use of the family car, permission to go to a party. Russians are more apt to withdraw love. A Soviet mother who considers promptness essential may say to her tardy son, "You've disobeyed me again. Now I don't feel like finishing the chess match we began yesterday; I don't even like to look at you."

In Communist China, punishment is considered an ineffective tool for socialization; a young child struggling to draw the elaborate characters of Chinese calligraphy finds that his mistakes are ignored and only his best work is noted. Crow Indians, on the other hand, emphasize punishment, and behavior the culture finds unacceptable is publicly ridiculed; a whole camp may come alive at night with shouts of derision directed at some unfortunate offender.

From culture to culture socialization seems everywhere different and yet the same, for while methods vary the goal is always the making of a human adult. Everywhere the family is a relatively small group of people devoted to bringing up children. Only small groups have succeeded in this purpose, although increasingly they are being challenged by large groups. Similarly, only groups whose purpose is raising children have succeeded. Beyond these constants of the family, there is no standard. The group may take almost any form, and it may fulfill its child-raising purpose in myriad bizarre ways.

If the small group forming a family consists simply of a man, a woman and their offspring, the unit is called a nuclear family, the familiar form in the West today. When members of a third or fourth generation join the two-generation nuclear household, the result is an extended family. It goes by other names—clan, kindred, patrilineage—when the group is larger or is constituted differently; it may center on one mother or several, one father or several, uncles, brothers or aunts. Anthropologists and historians have identified between 2,000 and 3,000 peoples with ways of life sufficiently different for them to be listed as distinct cultures. And each of these cultures has its own version of family life with its own goals, organization, ceremonies, strains and responses. Indeed, among the vast variety of shapes that family life has taken throughout the world, the 20th Century Western family counts as a special and almost eccentric case.

Whatever the form of the family, it exists for the sake of the children it produces and rears. And this fact may help explain the family's durability. For in assuring the survival of its children, it guarantees the continuation of the human species.

Album of an enduring family

The Lyon family of Massachusetts is living proof that the old-fashioned, tightly knit family survives and flourishes. The family album, which mirrors the experiences of many others who have lived during the same era, provides a four-generation record of the family as a resilient and enduring institution, one bound together by deep, unquestioning love, by pride in one another's accomplishments and in family history.

The Lyon family dates back in Massachusetts history to the 17th Century. The first Lyon, William, came to America in November 1635 on the *Hopewell*, one of the earliest ships after the *Mayflower*. He was an apprenticed armorer and farmer and lies buried in Roxbury.

The story depicted in the Lyons' family album centers on a direct descendant of this first settler, William Henry Lyon—known as "W. H." in the family —who was born in 1898 and died in 1963. He was the son of a Lexington farmer—also named William Henry Lyon—and Perla Coles of Fort Worth, Texas. Their wedding is recorded in the marriage certificate at right. W. H. became a well-known radio distributor and real-estate broker in the Boston area. He married Effie Prime of Nova Scotia and they had six children—three sons, William Henry, Robert and Richard, and three daughters, Dorothy, Judith and Elizabeth. To this family W. H. Lyon was the patriarch, the revered head-of-family in the 20th Century, and the Dad of the album. The role he played in strengthening a traditional family is indicated by the warmth of the captions, which, along with the moving expression of family purpose on this page, were written by his son, the present William Henry Lyon.

"My family, of which I am now uncomfortably patriarch, is held together principally by two things: by the love my parents always had for each other and all of us, and by a sense of history inculcated in us at such an early age that since childhood we have been very much aware that we are merely the current generation of a long and enduring success story. In a relay race one is urged not to drop the baton, and so it has been and will be from generation to generation; the baton will not be dropped. It is not an easy task nor is it free from tears and even hardships.

"One of my father's sadnesses was that I have no sons, and hence there will be no more William Henrys in direct succession. But brother Robert has a son and we all rejoice in this. Soon his hand will reach for the baton. We are confident that it will be a strong hand, and so The Family will continue.

"And what of my brothers and sisters? We support each other in adversity and against common foes, but otherwise we are all quite different personalities.

"My father's unspoken definition of Sin is one to which I also subscribe: if you do not rise to the fullest achievement of which you are capable, you desert those who made it possible for you. Strive, excel and lend a helping hand to those who cannot, and particularly those who may be in The Family."

William Henry Lyon

"Grandfather Lyon sits proudly with Aunt Doris, while Nana Lyon and Dad stand."

"Dad's other sister, Virginia, feeds some of Nana's chickens."

"Dad looks chipper and self-confident in his Sunday best, about 1905."

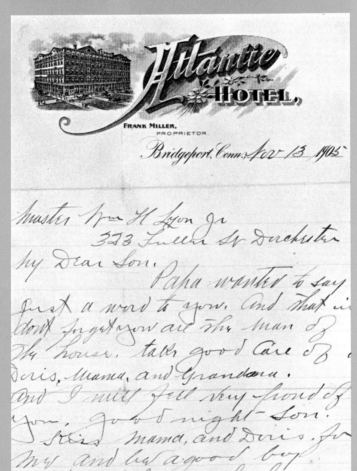

"Dad rides beside his father on a visit to Cheyenne Canyon, Wyoming, in 1908."

Grandfather Lyon, who appears in these pictures, was a strong family man. His warmth and love come through in the letter at left, written shortly before he died.

"Mom, seated fourth from right, wears a flowered hat and a stylish sailor tie for a touring-car outing on Nantucket before she married Dad."

"Dad's 1915 high-school graduation picture the year he became a radio operator."

"I'm on the left, then Dick and Bob, in this 1930 picture with Mom."

"Here's Dad with Dick, me in the middle, and Bob. Even at 12, I looked like Dad."

"During the Depression we lived for a time in this small house in Lexington."

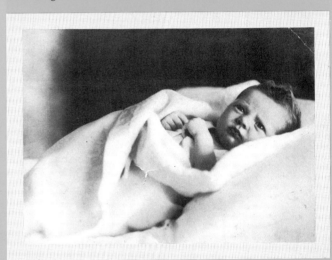
"At last a daughter, Dottie, 10 years younger than I, was born to the family in July of 1936."

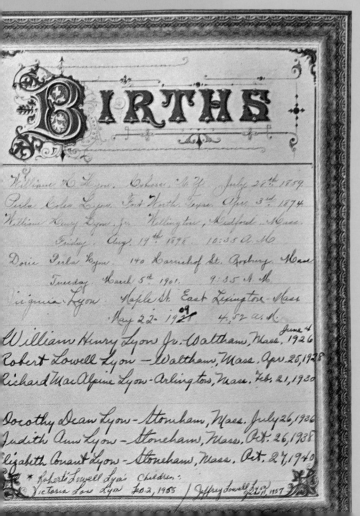

BIRTHS

William H. Lyon, Oswego, N.Y. July 28th 1859
Perla Coles Lyon, Fort Worth, Texas. Apr. 3rd 1874
William Henry Lyon, Jr. Wellington, Medford, Mass.
   Friday, Aug. 19th 1898, 10:35 A.M.
Dorie Perla Lyon, 140 Carruthof St. Roxbury, Mass.
   Tuesday, March 5th 1901, 9:35 A.M.
Virginia Lyon, Maple St. East Lexington, Mass.
   May 22, 1924, 4:52 A.M.
William Henry Lyon, Jr. Waltham, Mass. June 4, 1926
Robert Lowell Lyon – Waltham, Mass. Apr. 25, 1928
Richard MacAlpine Lyon – Arlington, Mass. Feb. 21, 1930
Dorothy Dean Lyon – Stoneham, Mass. July 26, 1936
Judith Ann Lyon – Stoneham, Mass. Oct. 26, 1938
Elizabeth Conant Lyon – Stoneham, Mass. Oct. 27, 1940
* Robert Lowell Lyon's Children:
Victoria Lou Lyon Feb 2, 1955, Jeffrey Lowell Sept 17, 1957

The marriage to Effie Prime of the W. H. Lyon who was family leader during the 20th Century is registered in the family Bible with the births of all their children. The pictures show what the elder Lyons were like before they were married and then during the years when they brought up a family. They had quite a struggle during the Depression with six children.

"In 1936 Dad started his real-estate business from this large house in Bedford."

"Bob was singing in the Episcopal Church choir in 1942; he's the tall one in the middle row on the left."

"Mom helps us feed the ducks on an outing at Norumbega Park in nearby Newton."

"My graduation from Boston University in the summer of 1950 was a happy occasion for Mom and Dad—and me."

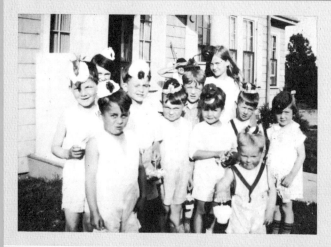

"My fourth birthday party. I'm second from the right, and my brother Bob is standing in front of me."

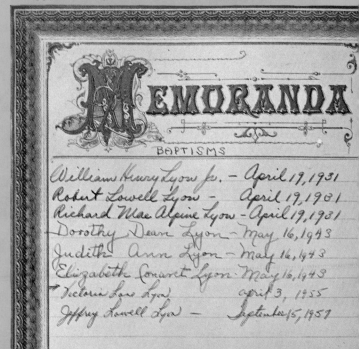

MEMORANDA

BAPTISMS

William Henry Lyon Jr. — April 19, 1931
Robert Lowell Lyon — April 19, 1931
Richard Mac Alpine Lyon — April 19, 1931
Dorothy Dean Lyon — May 16, 1943
Judith Ann Lyon — May 16, 1943
Elizabeth Conant Lyon — May 16, 1943
Victoria Lowe Lyon — April 3, 1955
Jeffrey Lowell Lyon — September 15, 1959

"This house on Oakland Street, Lexington, where we moved in 1944, was the family home we all remember best."

"Mom visits brothers Dick and Bob at Boy Scout camp. Dick loved camp; Bob hated it."

"During the Korean War when Dick and Bob were stationed at Camp Drum, New York, they met Mom on leave in Albany."

The baptisms of the present William Henry Lyon and his five brothers and sisters—plus those of Robert Lyon's two youngsters— are chronicled at left. Even during the years when they were at college or in the service the six Lyons kept in close touch with one another and went home to be with the family whenever they could.

" 'The happiest picture,' Mom says of this snapshot showing her with all six children at our Cape Cod summer home in 1948."

"Bob and Dolores enjoy a Cape Cod kiss shortly after their wedding was duly reported (below)."

"Dottie's wedding day in 1955. Dad was almost in tears as he prepared to give away his oldest daughter."

RECENTLY MARRIED — Mr. and Mrs. Robert Lowell Lyon
(Zitso Studio)

Miss Dolores Watson Weds Robert L. Lyon

At a 3 o'clock ceremony Sunday afternoon in the home of the bride's parents, Miss Dolores Ann Watson, daughter of Mr. and Mrs. Jennings B. Watson of 17 Carley rd., was united in marriage with Robert Lowell Lyon, son of Mr. and Mrs. W. H. Lyon of 24 Oakland st. Rev. Earl D. Haywood performed the single ring ceremony in a setting of white and pink flowers, and a reception followed at the Watson home.

"Dad bought this old farmhouse in Barnstable, on Cape Cod, in 1941, and fixed it up for a family summer place."

"Four generations celebrate Gram Prime's 82nd birthday in 1955: Gram holds her great-granddaughter Vicki."

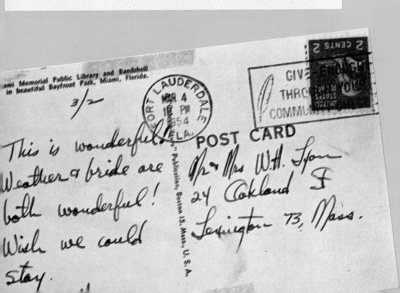

"My sister Betsy and Mom keep an eye on Mom's first grandchild, Bob's daughter Vicki, in Mom's Lexington house, 1956."

This is wonderful! Weather & bride are both wonderful! Wish we could stay.

Some of the family's happy times are recorded on these pages, including newspaper clippings of the weddings of sister Dottie and brother Bob, and a postcard from his honeymoon in Florida.

29

"Here I'm standing in front of portraits of some early 19th Century forebears of the Lyon family."

"Brother Bob and his son Jeff share a moment together at the wedding of our youngest sister, Betsy, in 1964."

"More grandchildren (my nieces): Dottie's girls Mary Jane and Debbie (left and right) with Dick's daughter Susie."

"Mom and Dad enjoy a happy moment with their poodle on their 37th wedding anniversary in 1962. Dad died during the next year.

30

"Grandchildren surround Mom during a birthday party for Judy's daughter Cynthia on Cape Cod in the summer of 1972."

"Brother Bob, who lives in this beautiful old house in Concord, carries on Dad's real-estate business."

Mary Jane Coles at Lexington, Mass. 1937
William H. Lyon at Lexington, Mass. Dec. 26, 1908.
Perla Coles Lyon at Lexington, Mass. Feb. 16, 1946
William Henry Lyon at Lexington, Mass. Oct. 8, 1963

William Lyon, Radio Pioneer

Private funeral services will be held in Douglass Chapel in Lexington for William H. Lyon, 65, of Oakland st., Lexington, a leading realtor and a pioneer in radio, who died in Emerson Hospital.

A lifelong resident of Lexington, he was licensed as a commercial radio operator in 1915 for the United Fruit Co. He later became the New England distributor for the major radio concerns of the period.

He was a member of the Boston Real Estate Board and a founder and past president of the Central Middlesex Multiple Listing Service.

A summer resident of Barnstable, he was an ardent tuna fisherman aboard his yacht

"Jeff, grown up now, accompanies his grandmother on a 1972 vacation trip to Portugal."

Every family knows sadness as well as happiness. The deaths of the first William Henry Lyon and his wife are registered at the left, along with that of their son, whose passing is also recorded in the obituary at left. The passing of the present William Henry, last of that name, will leave Jeff Lyon *(above)* as family patriarch.

A Solid Structure

Only a few generations ago, numerous social scientists, some of them esteemed authorities who should have known better, were proclaiming the unmatched virtues of the type of family common in the West, the "nuclear" arrangement of husband, wife and children. Men like Lewis Henry Morgan, intellectually captivated by Darwin's theory of biological evolution, constructed an evolutionary social theory: just as man developed by stages from the lowly primordial amoeba, so, these scientists reasoned, the modern Western family must have evolved from older, more primitive forms. Early man, hypothesized Morgan and some of his colleagues, lived in promiscuous hordes; his more enlightened descendants progressed to group marriage; and their successors in turn advanced at last to the civilized and ideal way of life typified by the monogamous nuclear family. The documentation intended to support this theory was elaborate. It was also incomplete and, to contemporary thinkers, is unconvincing.

Today anthropologists and sociologists know that evolutionary theories of the family are wrong, that the nuclear family does not represent an end product, a high point of development climaxing successive stages of advancement from lower to higher, or from primitive to civilized. The fact is that people have always lived in families, and the nuclear form of family organization appears to be as old as any other. Moreover, it is only one of many types of family structures that have coexisted throughout man's history. George Peter Murdock, whose work at Yale University made him one of the most respected students of family life, concluded that all these structures are variants of three basic forms; the nuclear family based on one husband and one wife; the polygamous family with a husband and several wives or a wife and several husbands; and the extended family, which may include as many relatives as the 14 parents, grandparents, brothers, sisters and cousins in the Hindu family at left. All three structures were found in ancient cultures, and all three exist today around the globe. None is morally superior or inferior to the others, none more civilized or more primitive, none inherently better or worse. They are simply different.

These variations in the membership of the family are not the only differences in the organization of the family. Size alone is an important factor: life in a traditional Chinese family of many years ago, which in some instances included 80 or more people, was far different from the everyday routine celebrated in the words of an American song of the '20s, "Just Molly and me and baby makes three . . ." The place where a newly married couple sets up housekeeping also influences the family pattern; in industrialized societies today, the bride and groom usually go off to live by themselves—perhaps the most ancient of all schemes, extending millions of years into the origins of human history—but elsewhere a new family often makes its home with the wife's relatives or with the husband's. The Dobuans, a dour people of the southwest Pacific, manage to make the worst of both worlds by requiring that every married couple spend alternate years in the native villages of wife and husband. Since these villages are inevitably in a state of permanent mutual hostility, each spouse is condemned to spend every other year in an atmosphere permeated with suspicion and malevolence. Yet the Dobuans apparently regard this hot-bed of strife as the normal setting for family life. Such "rules of residence" are bound up with "rules of descent," which determine whether the newly formed unit is to be considered an extension of the wife's family group or of the husband's—a matter of no small importance to society at large, for it affects not only the names children bear but also political alignments and the inheritance of titles and property.

All these distinctions in family organizations vary from place to place, culture to culture and time to time. Each variation has certain advantages under certain conditions; when conditions change so do some family patterns. Until now one pattern that has rarely changed much has been the division between husband and wife of responsibilities within the family; only today, as technical advances have everywhere eliminated many male biological advantages, have husbands and wives begun to share labors and authority more equitably between them. Women all over the world have gone outside the home to work, and increasingly they work side by side with men at the same jobs and for the same pay. Simultaneously, labor-saving devices, improved health measures and contraception have reduced the drudgery of family care at home. As a result, husbands cook and clean, wives provide financial support and both wear the pants in the family. This equal division of responsibilities is a radical change in a pattern that has endured perhaps since the long-ago days of the ape men. It is probably the most significant shift in family organization now taking place, but it is only one of the ways the family adapts so that it can fulfill its purpose of perpetuating the human race.

Although the three basic forms of family—nuclear, polygamous and extended—continue to exist around the world, a trend toward the nuclear pattern is obvious and not hard to understand. The independent nuclear family, being small, is relatively mobile, and is well suited to societies where one or both spouses may change work locations repeatedly. Such is the case in complex technological cultures, where the nuclear family has reached its most typical modern expression.

The need for mobility, however, is also great in the relatively simple cultures of hunters and gatherers, people who survive by capturing wild animals and fish and by collecting nuts, berries and edible plants. The pygmies of the Andaman Island forests—a people so primitive that they apparently did not know how to make fire when they were discovered by European explorers a couple of centuries ago—are monogamous. So too are the surviving Stone-age tribe of the Tasaday, discovered in 1971 in the mountains of the Philippine island of Mindanao. The Tasaday have no domestic animals, no permanent dwellings and no crops; they make fire by the friction of wood against wood and use crude tools of stone or bamboo. Despite this lack of sophistication, the Tasaday do not live in hordes, or even in large extended families. The basic family unit consists of husband, wife and unmarried children.

The mobile nuclear family has throughout history coexisted with the polygamous type. Even in the Western part of the world, where monogamy has long been at least the nominal rule, some people have set up polygamous families more or less openly. The liaisons among the nobility at European courts were notorious examples of this custom. During the 19th Century, many wealthy men maintained mistresses—and their homes and children—as second or even third "back-street" families. This practice seems to have practically disappeared, but it has been replaced by a new kind of "serial" polygamy that has been made possible by easy, repeated divorce followed by remarriage.

If monogamous societies have always included informal polygamy, the technically polygamous societies—which make up fully three fourths of the world—have always been largely monogamous. One reason is to be found in economics: it usually costs much more to maintain several households than to maintain just one, and extra spouses can be acquired only by the richer and more powerful members of the community. There are demographic reasons as well: in any given society, men and women are about equal in number, and it is a matter of simple arithmetic, therefore, that only a minority of men can have more than one wife. King Solomon's household of a thousand wives meant that 999 other men were doomed to the life of bachelors. In addition, the chances of strife and bickering, numerous enough in a single marriage, multiply alarmingly in a plural one. It is not surprising that with the spread of modern ideas of female independence, polygamy should seem to be on the way out, pushed along by the economic and social pressures of industrialization.

Yet in the past, and in some places today, polygamy has offered clear advantages to family stability. Rarely, if ever, has this form of family involved sexual promiscuity among several men and several women. Rather it matches one man with several women—polygyny—or less commonly, one woman with several men, in the arrangement called polyandry.

In many societies, having more than one wife is a mark of status. In others, it satisfies the prosaic need for extra help around the house or on the land. In a few instances, the motive is sexual. Among the Lango of East Africa, mothers nurse their children until they are three or four years old

Crouching in a cool mountain stream, a Tasaday mother bathes her baby. Child-rearing chores are shared by the husband and wife in the primitive community.

Family harmony in the Stone Age

Small families and communal living arrangements may seem like modern inventions, but are probably as ancient as any other style of family life. The evidence comes from a cave-dwelling Stone-age type of people called the Tasaday, in the jungle clad mountains of the Philippine Island of Mindanao.

The Tasaday combine the small nuclear family—mother, father and their children—with a communal decision-making process. Each family takes care of its own babies and gathers its own fuel. But all decisions—including marriage choices—are made jointly. So harmonious is their life that one expert terms the Tasaday "the gentlest people on the face of the earth."

Members of the Tasaday tribe perch on cave ledges in a densely forested area of Mindanao. Orphans and widows attach themselves to the nuclear families.

As a father munches on some wild fruit, his small son plays with a flower. The Tasaday parents usually maintain close contact with their young children.

Inside a cave the Tasaday cook a meal of frogs and grubs over open fires. Each family takes responsibility for gathering its own fuel and cooking its own food.

and are strictly forbidden to sleep with their husbands until weaning is over. Such prolonged abstinence is not expected of the men and they are allowed to marry several women so that one or another will be available most of the time. Among people whose ratio of men to women is out of balance because men are periodically slaughtered in wars, polygyny is intended to meet the sexual needs of females: if it were not permitted, some women would never have a chance of marriage at all. This line of reasoning has led quite a number of social planners to suggest optional polygyny for older members of Western cultures, in which women outlive—and therefore outnumber—men.

One example of an existing polygynous culture is that of the Kikuyu in East Africa, where the most prosperous men have several wives both to enhance their prestige and to do their farm and household chores. Conflict among these wives is said to be rare, and when it occurs the provocation is less often sexual jealousy than maternal pique over favoritism shown by the husband to the children of other wives. Among the Kikuyu, as among all polygynous peoples, multiple wives are less at the mercy of their husbands than it might seem. Ira Reiss, a sociologist at the University of Minnesota, points out that several wives can gang up on their one husband, backing their demands with more power than one wife is likely to be able to wield in a monogamous society.

In another polygynous society, the Central African Baganda tribe, husbands and wives live apart. To minimize wifely jealousy, the husband provides each wife with a house and garden of her own, and invites the women, one at a time, to come to his own house for visits. Conflict is further reduced by a system of clearly defined responsibilities. The first wife, outranking all her successors, looks after the family's religious fetishes, objects such as buffalo horns filled with herbs and clay and presumably inhabited by powerful spirits. The second wife is charged with shaving her husband's head, cutting his nails and then protecting the trimmings against enemies who might try to get them for use in death-dealing magic ceremonies. Additional duties are assigned to other wives.

Polyandry, which means the marriage of one woman to several husbands at the same time, is much rarer than polygyny. Only a tiny percentage of the world's population ever sanctioned this kind of family structure, and it has very nearly vanished today. Nevertheless, it was perfectly logical under certain conditions.

Among those who set up polyandrous families, the Nayar of the Malabar Coast of southern India practiced a remarkable variant that seemed to fly in the face of every code adhered to by other peoples. As soon as a girl reached puberty, she was married to a young man, preferably one of higher social station than herself, chosen by an astrologer. The bridegroom might or might not consummate his marriage. They did not expect him, however, to have anything more to do with the girl. She entered instead into a series of *sambandham* unions, meaning that she took a succession of equal or higher-caste husbands, sometimes really transitory lovers, who visited her only at night (leaving a quiver at the door to indicate that no one else need apply) and each of whom had no legal commitment except to bring a suitable gift of cloth if the union resulted in a baby whose paternity he chose to recognize.

All the children of this succession of fathers were brought up by the mother and her sisters in a large house that was ruled by the mother's eldest brother. The children addressed all the fathers, including the official husband of their mother, by the same title: *acchan*, lord.

These arrangements long scandalized observers from other cultures, and anthropologists gravely debated whether the words marriage and family could properly be applied to them. The Nayar certainly thought so; they took their rules very seriously, and would strangle any girl who broke them —if, for example, she slept with a man of inferior caste. Viewed in the context of the society in which they evolved, the rules made sense. The Nayars were a caste of professional soldiers, and all the young men were away fighting or training the greater part of the year. The family arrangements allowed them to have women when they returned on leave, and at the same time provided a stable home for the children. In recent days the social background has been transformed.

The Nayar men are no longer employed as mercenaries; they are fitting into more regular patterns of Indian life, and are tending to live in families whose structure seems less outlandish to Western observers. As a result Nayar polyandry has virtually disappeared.

A similar decline in popularity affected the third basic type of family, the extended family, in which three or more generations live under one roof. Only a few generations ago, it was the common type of family in the West, and it is still very much in evidence in many areas. One of the more unusual variants does not even include the father of the youngest generation. Among the Mentawei of West Sumatra, a typical household is made up of a set of grandparents, their sons and daughters, and their daughters' offspring. Each child, whose parents are unmarried at the time of his birth, is adopted by his maternal grandfather and supported by his maternal uncles. The child's father lives elsewhere, but when he reaches middle age, he marries his child's mother and adopts his own offspring. Less unusual are so-called stem families, like those in rural Ireland, where the father and mother live in the same household with a married son (who is usually the eldest) and his wife and children. Also fairly common are joint families like those established by some Hindus: a number of related men —generally they are either brothers or cousins—live together with their respective wives and children in their grandfather's house or compound. In this arrangement, all the members of the family share property, food and household goods alike.

Among the most extended of extended families was the Chinese family as it existed before the revolutions of the 20th Century. In a few households, 80 or more people might be living together: an old man and his wife and concubines, their unmarried sons and daughters, their married sons and their wives and children, perhaps their married grandsons and *their* children. In such a family, actions and attitudes were regulated by an elaborate code of behavior; it was so thoroughly indoctrinated into the young people that it became second nature to them. "Between husband and wife," said the ancient Chinese laws, "there should be attention to their separate functions; between father and son, affection; and between old and young, a proper order."

Orderly relationships among members of a family are obviously necessary, particularly in large extended families but to some extent in small ones as well. Each person has to know which of the family's duties he must perform and who performs the others. He must know who takes orders and who gives them, who is owed respect and who can be treated lightly, who can be depended on for help and who will turn to him. Some of these arrangements are, or at least were, almost universal: "Honor thy father and thy mother" is a commandment recognizable everywhere.

Some of the other notable rules of family life seem to depend somewhat on the type of family structure, but many of them are ancient traditions whose logic—if they ever had any at all—cannot now be perceived. Taken together, such relationships form organizational patterns that lie beneath the basic nuclear, polygamous and extended forms of family life.

The Walumba of North Australia, at least before the coming of the white man, were extended-type families living in a world where everyone they were apt to meet in the course of a lifetime was related to them by some tie. Every individual Walumba had his specific place in a web of kinship, which has been compared by Ronald Berndt of the University of Western Australia to "a map on which all the persons he knows have their places too, with more or less specific indications of his obligations toward them and what he can expect from them."

Such webs of kinship can become fantastically complex by Western standards. The Baganda of Central Africa need 68 principal kinship terms to sort out their close relatives, while English-speaking peoples get along with 13 (husband, wife, father, mother, brother, sister, son, daughter, aunt, uncle, niece, nephew, cousin). A Beduin of Cyrenaica would have difficulty understanding how a Westerner could confuse in the same category two individuals as different as his father's brother, a person of enormous authority demanding obedience and respect, and his mother's brother, with whom he is expected to exchange obscenities, horseplay and practical jokes. In the modern nuclear or extended family, both men would be called uncle and rated by their nephews and nieces on purely personal and emotional considerations (Who has the nicest smile? Who is going to leave me the most money?).

The nephews and nieces who ask themselves such questions may not realize, however, that even in their own modern cultures, tradition affects the answers. Ancient rules of descent may set patterns of allegiance and inheritance that determine what a person can expect from his mother's side

Polygamy was outlawed by the Mormon Church in 1890, but the practice continued until recently among many adherents. Morris Kunz, shown with his three wives, Ruth, Ellen and Margaret, defied the ban and went to prison in 1945 for two years rather than sign a statement disavowing polygamy.

Dapper in Western hat and blazer, the rich chief of the Ukuanjama tribe, Nehemia Chovalego, poses with some of his 18 wives and 38 children. The acute shortage of eligible men in many underdeveloped societies means that, for many African women, polygamy is the only kind of marriage they can hope for.

of the family and what from his father's side. In Western families today many aspects of descent are reckoned equally from the father's side and the mother's side. Choice or chance may bring a child closer to one set of grandparents, uncles, aunts and cousins than to the other, but legally he stands in the same relationship to both sides of the family, and neither outranks the other.

Even in the West, however, there are a number of interesting—and often socially important—exceptions to this evenhandedness. Generally a child takes his father's family name. Spanish-speaking peoples, however, use both—and the most famous artist of this century preferred to be known not by his father's name of Ruiz but by his mother's, Picasso. Jews take the father's name but their religion technically descends only from the mother, a fact that often causes turmoil in mixed marriages. An Israeli naval officer had to appeal to that country's supreme court to win citizenship for his two children, who were not Jews because their Scottish mother had not been converted to Judaism. Even in broad-minded America, most rabbis refuse to accept as a member of the congregation, in the traditional *bar mitzvah* ceremony, the son of a gentile mother. No matter how pious the Jewish father may be or how rigorous the boy's Jewish religious indoctrination, he is not a Jew unless his mother is Jewish either by birth or by conversion.

In some non-Western cultures, the connection to the maternal line is much closer and the father's side may be totally ignored—he may even be known by some such term as Mother's Husband. Most societies, however, orient families toward the father, particularly in the crucial matter of the inheritance of property and authority.

Under the system known as primogeniture, the father's property and power are inherited by his oldest surviving son, although in some instances the transfer does not work out the way it was expected to. Edward VIII did inherit the throne of England from his father in 1937 but ruled only 11 months, stepping aside in favor of his younger brother, George VI.

The Japanese *ie*, or stem family, deliberately makes primogeniture flexible: if the father thinks none of his sons is adequate for the job, he can adopt another young man of more humble origin, whose loyalties and commitments are then transferred *in toto* to his new family. It was by judicious use of this flexible device that the great Japanese merchant families, the *zaibatsu*, choosing their heirs the same way General Motors might choose a president, were able to keep their authority safely concentrated in able hands. This versatile control over leadership enabled them both to superintend and also to profit from the transformation of feudal-agrarian Japan into a capitalist-industrial state.

In lands where the paternal authority is less firmly entrenched than it is in Japan, the transition can be stormy. The history of the royal houses of Europe, which are extended families practicing primogeniture, is dotted with conspiracies and revolts by sons impatient to succeed to their father's honors. Witness the struggle of Richard the Lion-Hearted, for example, against his father Henry II. Strong emotions again came into play when Louis XIII of France on his deathbed asked his five-year-old son, "What is your name?" "Louis XIV, Papa," the boy replied. "Not yet," said the dying king bitterly.

Even among common folk the transfer of rights can be stormy. The rural family in Ireland lives, on the average, on a farm too small to be subdivided any further, and therefore only one son can inherit the land. The father can pick any one of them he likes, but he does not indicate his choice until he is good and ready. The result is that the sons who do not emigrate or drift off to jobs in the cities stay home and go on working, in a position of total subordination to the old man. And if they should get a side job like road mending, their wages are supposed to go into their father's pocket, and he is quite capable of turning up himself on payday to collect whatever money they may have earned.

Since marriage in the old-fashioned society of rural Ireland involves a property settlement, and the sons have no property, they may have to stay unmarried till they are in their fifties and older. When the old man is finally ready to retire and turn the farm over to a successor, he moves with his wife into the west room, the best in the house; the son of his choice is at last free to get married and start the cycle again, unless he has turned into a confirmed bachelor over the abstemious years.

These instances of turmoil over the transfer of rights in families all refer to struggles between sons and fathers. The rights contested have until now been male rights. Anthropologists have found no society where women are brought up to be dominant over men. There are some people, like the Hopi, among whom women seem to receive as much respect and enjoy as much authority as men. This female status exists in the spirit world as well: Hopi goddesses rank as high as Hopi gods.

In the overwhelming majority of societies, the man is unmistakably designated as ruler of the roost. In some, wives can be purchased with an appropriate number of cows or goats. In others—including Europe and the United States not too long ago—the rules of conduct, if not the laws, permitted the husband to kill his wife out of hand if he caught her in adultery; reciprocal privileges were rarely granted to the wife. The English common law, as it was expounded by the 18th Century jurist Blackstone, held that "a woman upon marriage dissolves her legal personality into that of her husband." Napoleon put the subordinate role of wives more crudely: "Woman is given to man to bear children; she is therefore his property, as the tree is the gardener's."

Male dominance and male authority do not necessarily, however, mean male power. In the most blatantly male-chauvinist world, a strong or a shrewd woman can get herself into the driver's seat, as far as the practical decisions of daily life are concerned. Sometimes, indeed, she is forced to take over control of family affairs by the very nature of the rules she and her husband live by.

Gathered for a reunion in Truro, Massachusetts, the 200-odd descendants of Cape Cod pioneer Richard Rich pose with the family coat of arms, then enjoy a clambake to celebrate the continuity of one of the oldest families in America.

Consider, for example, the orthodox Jewish communities, the *shtetls*, of Eastern Europe before World War I. There the pious husband began his day by thanking God for not having made him a woman. He alone had access to the most precious possessions of the people, for it was he alone who could read and expound the Law of God. The more pious he was, the more time he would spend studying and debating the finer points of commentaries on the books of Moses. He was admired for his pale complexion, "revealing long hours spent over books . . . deepset semiclosed eyes, indicating weariness from constant poring over texts . . . pale delicate hands, evidence that the owner has devoted his life to exercise of the mind rather than of the body."

It is obvious that the closer any man came to this ideal, the less capable he was of handling the family business, not to speak of all the practical problems and human contacts of the noisy, stifling little town

where his family had to survive. The wife had to take over, and in her liberated Americanized descendant she became the bighearted, overprotective Jewish Mother who is a stock figure of recent fiction. To an outside observer, such a matriarch would appear unquestionably to be the most powerful figure in the family, but of course the *shtetl* did not live by the standards of outside observers. In its own terms the husband was the dominant figure: to him alone was accorded the right to sit by the east wall of the synagogue.

Similar ambiguities crop up when social scientists attempt to measure the relative power of husbands and wives in modern urban communities. There have been many studies in the United States designed to determine which spouse makes the final decision in a variety of actions that concern the family as a whole. The husband almost always has the last say when it comes to choosing the make of car to buy (though it is no surprise that the wife generally picks the color). The wife ordinarily has the final word when it comes to expenditures for food or for medical care, and the two share responsibility on matters like vacations. Since in the current American scheme of things, jobs and automobiles generally carry far more prestige than do food and drugs, it is concluded that the balance of power in the family is tipped toward the masculine end of the scale.

Such distinctions in what each spouse does in a family almost certainly arose because of what each sex can do. In the first place, men are stronger than women, although physical strength has never been as crucial a factor as many people believe. Outside of the uppermost classes, women work at least as hard as men. Eskimo women hunt walruses. Soviet women build dams. And in the Western world, too, women were driven rather hard in the fairly recent past. An English handbook of the 17th Century describes the duties of a yeoman's wife as follows: " . . . to winnow all manner of corns, to make malt, wash and wring, to make hay, shear corn, and in time of need to help her husband to fill the muck wain or dung cart, drive the plough, to load hay, corn and such other . . . ," as well as to sell dairy products, fowl and pigs at the market. And although this list of tasks may suggest otherwise, a yeoman's wife was fairly high up on the social scale of the times.

More significant than any muscular deficiency was the fact that the woman was periodically incapacitated by pregnancy, childbearing and nursing. In the days before scientific birth control and antiseptic delivery, the children came repeatedly, and many if not most of them died. The gentle complaint of Mrs. Clapp, wife of the President of Yale in the middle of the 18th Century, echoes down the ages from a letter of her husband's. "Indeed she would sometimes say to me that bearing, tending and burying children was hard work, and that she had done a great deal of it for one of her age (she had six children, whereof she buried four, and died in the 24 year of her age)."

Tied to her children, the wife's duties naturally gravitated around the hearth where the children had to be kept warm and fed, while the man could wander farther afield. Thus arose a distinction that the Koreans recognize to this day; their common term for husband is Outside Boss, for wife, Inside Boss. In some cultures, like the traditional Japanese, the different roles of men and women were so carefully spelled out by custom that most family activities did not require active decision-making by either husband or wife.

In three fourths or more of the societies for which information is available, women are expected to carry out tasks like these: grinding grain, carrying water, cooking, preserving food, repairing and making clothing, weaving, gathering food, making pottery. The men are assigned tasks like these: herding, hunting and fishing, lumbering, mining and quarrying, metalworking and housebuilding. The distinction is still felt in the nuclear family of modern suburbia, where the husband usually shovels the snow and mows the lawn, while the wife more often than not is responsible for doing the evening dishes and straightening up the living room when company is coming.

How these distinctions in roles may influence the division of authority in a family is suggested by a study made by Robert Bales in 1947. He was interested in the leadership of small groups, and worked out an ingenious experiment involving 30 five-man groups of Harvard freshmen. Each group was given a task to perform in common, and watched closely while its members did their best to accomplish it. In almost every case, Bales found, two distinct leaders arose, exercising two distinct types of leadership. One, the "instrumental leader," took charge, set goals and provided the drive to get things done. The other, the "expressive leader," set the tone, kept the proper atmosphere and enabled the group to work together harmoniously. Many sociologists argue that this scheme applies to the conventional nuclear family. As breadwinner the husband-father is the instrumental leader, providing for his family and establishing its status in society. As homemaker the wife-mother is the expressive leader. A study conducted at Harvard led Talcott Parsons and Renee Fox to conclude that she acts as "skillful mediator of the child-father relationship and thereby assures both the perpetuation of family solidarity and the emotional security of the child."

It may well be asked at this point: Why does the wife have to play the expressive role alone? Why should she not take the instrumental one as well? Can both roles be shared by husband and wife? These questions have indeed been asked, with greater or less passionate indignation, by women throughout history. But for a long time the questions about the family roles of men and women were largely academic.

Only in the past century or so has it been possible to speak seriously of equality between the sexes, because only then was it possible to begin removing some of the handicaps under which women have labored. Muscular effort is no longer a premium in modern life, and the male's bigger biceps now give him no special advantage. Modern medicine and liberalized abortion laws have ended the necessity for the unending round of births that distressed and prematurely killed poor Mrs. Clapp. It is precisely here that the principal revolution in modern family structure has taken place: For the first time in human history the family can control its size in accordance with its wishes and interests, freeing the wife, if she so desires, to work alongside men on a basis of equality.

Revolution in the family can take place with truly revolutionary speed —but only if conditions demand it. In China, for example, a powerful Communist regime supports a family structure that retains much of the warmth and strength of imperialist tradition, yet has been radically changed by governmental pressure in other ways, particularly in the status granted female members.

Many experts confidently predicted that when the Communists took over China, they would break their teeth on the ancient family structure, which had survived so many shocks of history and changes of dynasty in the previous 2,000 years and more. But this edifice had weak spots, which the new masters shrewdly attacked. One of them was the misery and resentment of the young married woman. By immemorial custom she had to come from a different *tsu* or clan from her husband's (which, in practice, almost always meant a different village or a different quarter of the city), and she had to go to live in a strange household dominated by the fierce figure of her husband's mother, who probably had many humiliations of her own in her past to live down. "The cruel mother-in-law in Chinese fiction and folklore," says one authority, "plays the role that the wicked stepmother plays in European fairy tales." In former times, when flight and divorce were usually impossible, the only possible responses for an unhappy bride were to submit or else to commit suicide. The records of the city of Peking for 1917 contain one of those odd little statistical figures that unexpectedly illumine the darker corners of life: In the age group between 21 and 30 years, when for the average young woman the bloom of marriage had worn off and she was raising her first children, the suicide rate among females was three and a half times as great as it was among males.

To millions of downtrodden wives the Communist rise to power must have seemed like a blessing that would break the power of the mother-in-law. It did. The status of the wife in the Chinese family changed sharply, and today resembles that of Western women.

The Chinese example is an exception. Generally, the family adapts to changes in its situation much more slowly, rarely discarding old patterns completely and most often modifying them gradually and conservatively over several generations. A convenient opportunity for observing the impact of new living conditions on traditional family structure has been provided by the waves of immigration to the United States from southern and eastern Europe during the decades before World War I. In this period the immigrants, coming mostly from agricultural regions, were

conservative, slow-moving, "disciplined," in one observer's words, "to the idea that the major decisions of the individual's life ought to be made in accordance with the aims and good of the group as a whole as defined by the oldest active member of the family." The American society into which they were drawn was, on the contrary, urban, individualistic, innovative, scornful of the past, oriented toward youth. Each successive ethnic group met the shock of change, and despite talk of the melting pot has kept a remarkable degree of identity up to the present. But each group has changed its way and its outlook, and the family ideals of today are often quite different from those of the original immigrants.

In the 1930s, a series of interviews probed the attitudes of women in the Little Italy of New York City, contrasting those of women over 35 (who were presumed to have been born in the old country) and those who were younger (and presumably born in America). While 30 per cent of the first group accepted marriages arranged by the parents of the bride and groom, only 1 per cent of the second did so. Fifty-two per cent of the older women sanctioned large families, against 14 per cent of the younger. Only 12 per cent of the older ones approved of divorce, compared with 39 per cent of the younger. And these figures apply only to the first two generations of Italian-Americans. In the third and fourth, the changes become more pronounced.

Attitudes that are reflected by sociological studies like the one of Italian-Americans may change far more rapidly than does actual practice. Such fundamental patterns of family life as size, for instance, seem to undergo alteration very slowly indeed.

The large size of families of the past is widely accepted without question. Indeed, numbers were one of the chief advantages of the extended type of family, the most common form in many areas until recently. A large family finds it easier to achieve economic self-sufficiency than a small one: When there are many relatives living together on a cooperative basis, it is always easy to find a baby sitter, a carpenter or some one to give a hand with the harvest—all services for which the nuclear family has to pay hard cash. And, of course, numbers give security; a large extended family is much better able to protect itself in unsettled times than is a small nuclear one. Even in peaceful eras, a large number of people living together under one roof provides homemade, womb-to-tomb social insurance. When any member of the family falls sick or grows old, there is someone else standing by who can assume his duties, take care of him and eventually bury him.

These advantages of the large extended family are remembered fondly by many Europeans and Americans, who recall the sense of security contributed to their childhood—or to their parents' childhood—by the presence at home of grandfather or of Aunt Mary. But this view is often grossly distorted by time and distance, for there is much misapprehension in the popular mind about the size of families in the past of Western countries as well as in foreign lands.

People speak of the swarming families of China and India, and sure enough their birth rates are high. But the number of people living together in one household is not necessarily—and in fact not usually—large, for children die, and many of those who live are obliged to leave home early in order to find work. Surveys in these Asian countries show relatively few persons in each household—the average is 3.5 to 5.5. This is not merely a feature of modern days. Families of 80-odd persons living under one roof were rare in any society, and almost surely restricted to the very uppermost classes. The expenses of construction on such a scale, not to speak of the servants needed to keep up such a household, could be met in China only by the landed gentry and rich merchants, who constituted a tiny fragment of the total population. The historian Peng-ti Ho cites a respectable census of the year 2 A.D. that indicates the number of persons in each household averaged 4.87.

So it is with the old days in the West. Americans tend to think of their ancestors as living in large farmhouses with several generations working harmoniously side by side. This is partly an optical illusion. As Columbia sociologist William Goode notes, the big houses, being better built, are the only ones that have survived, while the cabins where most people lived have long since rotted away or burned. When the first United States census was taken in 1790, the median figure for the persons in an American household was 5.7; nearly two centuries later, in 1965, the count was 3.7. Since the earlier figure includes domestic servants and lodgers, two categories that have virtually disappeared from contemporary society, the disparity is far less than might be supposed.

Such statistics seem to prove that family size has indeed changed, as everyone thought, but it has not changed nearly as much as everyone thought. The same conclusion applies to the bonds that unite family members. Social critic Vance Packard, noting the way modern Americans drift restlessly across the landscape, uprooting themselves from job and home so many times in the course of a lifetime, thinks that this mobility implies the dissolution of all the traditional ties holding families and society together. He sees mankind turning into what the zoologist Desmond Morris calls "a mass of strangers masquerading as members of our tribe."

There is considerable dissent from such a gloomy view. Many family members, even in generally mobile societies, show a marked tendency to stay in close proximity. An international study in 1968, covering cities in the United States, England and Denmark, revealed that more than 50 per cent of older people with married children lived within 30 minutes' travel time of at least one of them. Even separated family members may keep in touch. During the 1950s, sociologists began asking specifically how much contact people in modern urban communities maintained with their kin. The results were surprising, at least to the sociologists. They showed that an overwhelming majority of the people surveyed in widely separated communities—in the United States, England, Sweden, Poland—kept up a more or less constant and active give-and-take relationship with a network of parents, in-laws and cousins. Almost everyone, it turned out, made regular telephone calls to relatives; almost everyone made regular visits. A good three quarters turned to relatives first when they needed help, as in cases of serious illness. More than half made fairly regular gifts of money, and about the same number provided services like caring for children. About a third relied on relatives for advice on business and personal affairs. When the people surveyed were asked to check their favorite forms of recreation, the largest vote went to "visiting with relations."

The same considerations apply to social mobility. Few people rise in the world by their own unique efforts, unaided by cash and encouragement from kin. The poor boy who made good after his parents slaved to put him through college may well be contributing to the education of deserving nieces and nephews. Investigations of large groups by Bert Adams in Greensboro, North Carolina, and Elizabeth Botts in London cast doubt on the popular notion that people who rise on the social ladder snoot the relatives they have left behind on a lower rung. In both places, blue-collar workers who had succeeded in rising to white-collar status continued to keep up active relations with their network of kin, perhaps a little less than before their rise, but nevertheless more than the average of the middle-class communities they had moved into.

The enduring power of family bonds suggests the way the family may be evolving. It adapts to life in a technological age by taking advantage of the freedom of choice that technology offers. There is less emphasis on formal structure dictating who is to do what to whom and for whom. The distinctions between male and female roles blur. People visit their relatives on the basis of which ones they get along with best, not on the basis of a technical tie of genealogy. There is often a conscious effort to avoid anything that might smack of compulsion—parents may make costly, even extravagant gifts to grown children on birthdays or Christmas, but they avoid sending weekly or monthly checks.

These changes do not weaken the ancient strengths of the family. In all its forms, it remains the support of its members, the essential institution for the survival of the human race. It is still the "place where, when you go there, they have to take you in."

The Meaning of Marriage

There is one universal custom attached to the family: a wedding. Every culture recognizes the institution of marriage, and it sets rules, often rigid and elaborate, for matching spouses appropriately. In most cases it specifies some kind of exchange of gifts as a necessary preliminary. And it prescribes certain formalities—gestures or words or ceremonies—that make public and acceptable the fact that a man and a woman intend to live together and start a family.

The formalities attending marriage may be of the skimpiest. When a Kwoma woman in New Guinea approves of the girl her son has been sleeping with, she gets the young woman to prepare a bowl of soup and then offers it to the unsuspecting youth, who assumes that the cook was, as usual, his mother or one of his sisters. When his mother tells him the truth, the boy is expected to spit out the soup and say, "Faugh! It tastes bad. It is cooked terribly." By then it is too late: he is hooked; he is now a husband.

On the other hand the ceremonies that are the prelude to family life may be lavish and complicated, as they once were among the Kwakiutl Indians of the Northwest American Coast. In the 19th and early 20th centuries, the prospective fathers-in-law of a betrothed Kwakiutl couple were required to put on potlatches, feasts lasting three or four days in the course of which each man gave away or sometimes even burned enormous quantities of his most precious possessions—candlefish oil, blankets, canoes—in order to prove that his family was richer and more distinguished than that of his future relations.

Many modern European and American wedding ceremonies seem as lavish as those of the Kwakiutl. The daughters of these families take for granted festivities on a scale that would not have been out of place at the court of Marie Antoinette. The bride's dress, perhaps copied from a creation by a world-famous designer, may have cost hundreds of dollars. The prolonged ceremony may take place in a solemn religious setting before a dozen or more wedding attendants and scores of onlookers, to be followed by an elaborate reception featuring champagne and caviar. This already complex rite will be further elaborated with reminders of its ancient origins: a gold ring symbolizing the husband's right of possession, rice and confetti recalling prehistoric fertility rites, and sometimes, in the United States, noisy tin cans attached to the going-away car in an echo of the shivaree, the old-fashioned custom of making the night hideous with howls and firecrackers outside the window of a just-married pair.

All this festivity indicates the importance that people the world over set upon marriage. The formation of a family is, of course, a great turning point, a setting forth on a new and unpredictable course in life. Understandably it deserves notice. But why it must be noticed publicly and formally is not nearly so clear. A man and woman can, of course, live together and raise children without being married. And yet every society expects them to be. Marriage, it seems, fulfills some basic human purpose, one that is the same in the most advanced society or on the remotest South Sea island. The nature of that purpose was not fully explained until World War I, when it was studied under unlikely circumstances by the great Polish anthropologist Bronislaw Malinowski.

At the start of the war, Malinowski was in Australia and, as a citizen of the Austro-Hungarian Empire, subject to internment as an enemy alien. He asked and was given permission to move to the distant British colony of the Trobriand Islands in the southwest Pacific. The Melanesian people there, untouched as yet by the civilization that was to be brought them a generation later by World War II bombers and torpedo boats, were living in a Stone-age culture. These Trobrianders allowed free, random intercourse among their children when they reached puberty. Even the adults apparently did not know that the sexual act had anything to do with childbearing. And yet they insisted that a girl find a husband as soon as she became pregnant, and they were as devoted to the institution of marriage as any other people on earth. Why, with their beliefs, did they need marriage at all?

Malinowski's conclusion, set forth in his classic book *The Sexual Life of Savages,* is one that most subsequent scholars have agreed with: the primary function of marriage is to produce legitimate children, that is, children who have a name and place assigned them in the community. This stipulation means that a child must be connected, however tenuously, with both parents and with his parents' families. The mother, having borne the child, can hardly escape being tied to it; it is difficult to conceal a pregnancy and a birth. Marriage ensures that the father, too, will be publicly recognized as such.

The word "father" is ambiguous in many languages, including English, as any adopted child knows. Anthropologists prefer to split the meaning between two Latin words: *progenitor,* the man whose seed produces the child, and *pater,* the head of the family, the man who brings the child up, the "sociological father." Malinowski's Principle of Legitimacy holds that "no child should be brought into the world without a man assuming the role of sociological father," needed to guarantee the child a proper place in his society.

Occasionally, through some odd semantic acrobatics, the provision of a proper pater requires a marriage between people of the same sex. Woman-woman marriages are recognized among the Nuer of East Africa, a matrilineal tribe in which property descends through the female line. If

בששי

Marriages may be made in Heaven, but
—as this 1775 Jewish marriage contract,
or Ketubah, makes clear—they are
formalized on earth. The antique document
states that the husband give his wife
"two hundred silver zuzim," an obsolete
coin, and that all his property, "even
the mantle on my shoulders," will be
mortgaged to secure the payment.

a rich woman finds herself sterile and lacking a child to carry on her family, she may marry another, younger woman, who afterward gets herself
with child by a man of her choice. The older woman is then considered the
pater of the resulting child; he refers to her as his father, receives her
name and inherits her property.

Kwakiutl legitimacy rules provided on occasion for marriage between
two men. The law in this tribe required a chief to be succeeded by his son-in-
law. But suppose he had no daughter? An ingenious solution was
developed. The chief simply married off one of his sons to the man he
thought best qualified for the job of chief, and thus became pater to this fic-
titious son-in-law, who eventually inherited the title. Meanwhile, this child-
designate was free to contract a second, normal, marriage with a woman
from another family and to produce daughters who would provide him
with sons-in-law to carry on the chiefly line. If he had only male children,
he could arrange another all-male marriage like his own.

In these same-sex as well as in conventional man-woman unions, the institution of marriage contributes to social stability by enabling families to reproduce themselves according to the ancient rules and customs on which the cohesion of a people depends, and without denying legitimate status to any children. For on youngsters born outside of marriage, society is generally harsh. It calls them bastards, subjects them to scorn or at least to subtle insult, and may deny them the right to inherit. "Why bastard? Wherefore base?" asks Edmund, the illegitimate son of Gloucester in *King Lear.* "When my dimensions are as well compact, / My mind as generous and my shape as true/ As honest madam's issue?" Quite so, but it is the legitimate Edgar who inherits Gloucester's name and lands.

Although all cultures prescribe a primary form of marriage that legitimizes children, some societies, taking account of human frailty, recognize an additional, alternate form of marriage that is sufficient to give children accepted status of some sort, a kind of secondary legitimacy. In England and America, this alternative is known as common-law marriage, the union of a man and woman without civil or religious ceremony, but simply as a result of their living together. Sociologists call this arrangement consensual union, and in some areas, such as Trinidad, this form of marriage may be dominant.

Trinidadians refer to consensual union as "living," said to be short for living in sin, since the Caribbean Islanders who participate in such arrangements have not solemnized their marriage before the authorities of either church or state. Some Trinidadians consider unions of this kind morally wrong. But in a majority of cases, the partners in living feel no sense of sin. They live together openly, and everyone understands why. In their part of the world, male employment is seasonal and precarious, so that the average young man, even if he has the inclination to marry, lacks the money to pay for a wedding ceremony and to take on the married man's role of permanent breadwinner for wife and children. Although the young woman does not necessarily like the living arrangement and would prefer to be married, she makes the best of what she has. She consoles herself with sayings like "Better a good living than a bad marriage," and with the hope that over the years her man will be able to scrape together enough money so that the two can spend their later years as a properly and conventionally married man and wife.

While the legitimization of children is the principal function of marriage, there are, of course, other important functions, relating not to the rights of children but to the feelings of husbands and wives. In many cultures, marriage provides each spouse with exclusive or preferential sexual rights to a partner, and it also offers the chance of a lifelong, mutually supporting, loving companionship. The importance of these secondary marital functions varies immensely from culture to culture, as well as within any particular culture. Love, or the whole complex of feelings—passionate longing, tenderness, closeness, mutual understanding and illumination—that goes under that name, may be regarded as decisively important, or it may count for nothing.

It has been said that only in the Polynesian islands and in the United States is love considered sufficient reason for getting married, and even in America it may be doubted whether all the love people talk about is genuine and not a more or less conscious imitation of the movies and other cultural pacesetters. The anthropologist Ralph Linton has written that "the hero of the modern American movie is always a lover, just as the hero of the old Arab epic is always an epileptic. A cynic might suspect that in any ordinary population the percentage of individuals with a capacity for romantic love of the Hollywood type was about as large as that of persons able to throw genuine epileptic fits. However, given a little social encouragement, either one can be adequately imitated without the performer's admitting even to himself that the performance is not genuine."

Margaret Mead notes that in New Guinea there is no word for love, and no understanding of the concept. In many cultures, love before marriage is viewed as a positive disaster, an irruption of anarchic human passion into the efforts of man to create a decent and orderly existence for himself and his family. The code of the Yi family, which reigned in Korea until the Japanese annexation of 1910, specifically declared a love marriage to be illegitimate and required that severe punishment be meted out to the participants. But most cultures proceed on more humane principles and encourage some degree of affection, or at least harmony, between spouses. One prominent authority on the family, William Goode, maintains that the capacity for love is universal, though it may be encouraged or tolerated or suppressed as the case may be by societies with a particular ax to grind in the matter.

In those societies that prize love between husband and wife, its role in marriage is often misunderstood. Most people will say they "married for love," implying that they chose their mates almost entirely on the basis of whether or not they loved them. Not even in movie-struck America is this generally the case. Love may be involved in the choice of a marriage partner, but rarely is it the only or even the most important factor. Mate selection is such a crucial preliminary to marriage that it is subject to many restrictions and requirements, some so peculiar to a particular society that they are obvious while others are so taken for granted that they may easily be overlooked.

One restriction on the choice of a spouse is seldom given a second thought because it is the oldest as well as the only one that is universal: the incest taboo, the absolute prohibition against sexual relations within one's immediate family. As applied to marital choice, the incest taboo takes the form of what social scientists call exogamy, the obligation to marry outside certain rigidly defined degrees of relationship.

The reasons for the origin and maintenance of the ban on incest pose one of the most vexing problems in anthropology, one that is far from solved. The idea that exogamy was enforced to prevent the inbreeding of ge-

This radiant Swedish couple, celebrating
their golden anniversary beneath their
wedding photograph, may be members of a
vanishing species. Certainly such
lifelong partnerships are becoming rarer,
and even the formation of legal unions is
declining in some countries. Between 1966
and 1971 the number of marriages in
Sweden dropped by a startling 35 per cent.
Many Swedish couples are simply
living together—in 1971 more than 20 per
cent of all the children born in Sweden
were the progeny of unmarried parents.

netic defects is now discounted, since the incest ban predates—perhaps by millions of years—any recognition of its influence on inherited abnormalities. More likely, exogamy guaranteed social stability. Sexual rivalry between father and son or brother and brother would have kept incestuous families in a constant uproar, perhaps leading to bloodshed, and at all events inhibiting cooperation and draining energies otherwise available for cultural development. More important, if the first human families had turned entirely in on themselves for marriage, they would probably have had no reason to establish peaceful communication with neighboring families. The incest taboo made it necessary to live on friendly terms, at least temporarily, with some outsiders so that spouses could be exchanged with them. Since man is a weapon-bearing animal with none of the built-in checks that keep dogs, lions and other animals from killing their own kind, the human family unrestrained by an incest ban might early on have extinguished itself in mutual slaughter.

So deeply ingrained is the incest taboo that for the average man the question of origin is irrelevant; he will say he loathes incest because it is contrary to the laws of God and Nature, and let it go at that. Perhaps it is; but if so, God and Nature have spoken with remarkably different voices to different peoples. Virtually everybody draws the line at sexual relations between sons and mothers. On fathers and daughters, there is a shade less unanimity. According to one authority, an African tribe called the Thonga allows such mating when the father is a mighty hunter and big game is in sight. Between siblings, there is still more latitude. The Pharaohs of ancient Egypt and the royal Incas of Peru married their sisters because they wanted to make sure that the throne stayed in the same family. And evidence has recently turned up of brother-sister marriages among commoners in the ancient kingdoms of Egypt and Persia. These are exceptional cases, however; most societies are united in frowning on relationships of this kind, differing mainly in how far they push the incest prohibition beyond the confines of the nuclear family to include a constellation of aunts and uncles, cousins and in-laws.

Rarely is the constellation of forbidden mates the same: what is unthinkable crime for one society may be tolerated or recommended behavior for another. "The Shilluk," observes anthropologist George Peter Murdock, "wink at affairs with a stepmother, and the Baiga at those with a maternal aunt, while the Trobrianders positively encourage them with a paternal aunt. The Tupinamba permit sex relations with a wife's niece, the Kaingang with a fraternal niece, the Bari with the mother's brother's wife, the Lepcha with the father's brother's wife."

Some societies have complicated the rules defining incest and regulating exogamy to an extreme degree. Consider the Purum, a tribe living on the eastern borders of Assam in India. In 1932 only 303 Purum existed, and they were divided into five exogamous clans. Everyone had to marry outside his clan, but no one was permitted to marry just *any* outsider. The five clans were further divided into 13 lineages, some of which could give

wives only to certain others, some of which could receive wives only from certain others. Thus, a male member of the Rimphungchong lineage of the Marrim clan could choose a wife only from the two lineages of the Kheyang clan and the Kankung lineage of the Makan clan. His sisters, on the other hand, could marry only men of the Makan-te lineage of the Makan clan and the Parpa clan (which mercifully had only one lineage).

Pushing things just a little further could make marriage a virtual impossibility, and that step was taken by the Kurnai of Australia. The rules in this tribe became so complicated that a boy coming to manhood was apt to find no permissible mate available. Every single girl of the group from which he had to choose a bride either was already bargained for by another, older man, or was technically classified as his sister. The rules were passionately believed in—they were the basis of the people's existence —yet if they were followed the people would die out. Ingenuity amended the rules enough for survival. The solution: A young couple would elope. The community would set out in hot pursuit, and if it caught the pair, would kill them out of hand—despite the fact that all the pursuers might have eloped themselves when they were younger. But if the couple could reach a certain island and stay there until the birth of their first child, they could come home and, after submitting to a good beating, take up their place in the community as legitimately married adults.

The rules of exogamy represent only one side of the general restrictions on mate selection. If every marriage is exogamous, there is a sense in which every one is also endogamous, that is, contracted *within* a more or less strictly defined group or population. While the rules of exogamy are nearly always rigid, those of endogamy tend to be rather flexible, enforced, if at all, less often by law than by custom, convenience and personal choice.

The in-group from which a marital partner is likely to be chosen may be defined in the first place by simple geography. Hottentot boys do not in the natural course of things marry Eskimo girls, because there is never any contact between the two societies. Romeo's love flashed into his life like a bolt of lightning, and young lovers to this day believe that the same thing has happened to them. It is odd, however, that this lightning should fall so often on the girl next door.

Statistical backing for the importance of proximity comes from the investigations of two sociologists, W. R. Catton and R. J. Smirchich, in Seattle in 1961. They checked all 413 marriage licenses granted in August of that year and plotted the applicants' addresses on a map of the city. By far the largest category of couples, the researchers found, lived within half a mile of each other, and there was a steady decline in the number of planned marriages as distances increased. The reason, Catton and Smirchich speculate, is that people have only a limited amount of time and energy to spend on love and courtship, and it is far easier and more economical to spend that time and energy on someone who lives nearby.

Geographical proximity is only one—and not necessarily the most important—of the factors in endogamy. People who are close together in space may still be separated by differences in caste, race, religion, age and life style. These differences tend to become barriers; every study on the subject shows that an overwhelming majority of people who get married find mates from their own cultural, racial, religious and social groups.

In India, for instance, the 1949 repeal of a centuries-old law prohibiting intercaste marriages did not change things much in practice; more than 90 per cent of men who married still chose wives from the caste into which they themselves were born. And while the United States Supreme Court in 1967 nullified all laws banning interracial marriage, such unions remain rare despite the country's melting pot tradition, and all but a tiny fraction of Americans choose spouses of their own race. Similarly, a great

continued on page 67

*Malays from Singapore play tambourines
and hold an umbrella—a sign of honor—
over the blue-garbed bridegroom as
they escort him to the house of the bride.*

Weddings around the world

The Malay bridegroom is accompanied by a procession of solicitous friends *(above)*. The Moscow couple takes a bus to a 10-minute civil ceremony. A royal princess commands a cathedral full of nobility and a fortune in jewels. The ceremonies are different, but the purpose is the same: a wedding to establish that a new family is being formed. There is a ceremony everywhere. Only its form and its attendant festivities vary, as colorful and distinctive as the society in which it occurs.

In India the wealthy Jaipur prince rides to his bride's house astride a hand-painted elephant, attended by an elaborate entourage, with music by bagpipes, drums and flutes. The ceremony takes place under a flower-bedecked canopy, and the bride and groom are joined together before a sacred fire with priests and family in attendance.

Among the Hopi Indians in the U.S. Southwest, wedding rites are lighthearted and gay. The hair of the wedding couple is washed in separate bowls of yucca suds. Then the suds are poured into a single bowl and the couple put their heads in together; their hair is mingled and tied together.

Even among people as poor as the Bugti tribe of Pakistan, the preparations are elaborate. The bride wears a red wedding dress embroidered with traditional tribal designs, and her palms and the soles of her feet are stained with henna. And after the ceremony, shooting competitions and camel and horse races celebrate the start of a family and the renewal of human society itself.

A wedding in a Turkish village is celebrated for at least three days, but the bride is seen only for a brief moment, when, veiled in the proper Muslim way, she is escorted by her brother and her father-in-law to the groom's house.

In Japan's Shinto wedding the bride traditionally wears an ornate white hat. The hat derives from a legend that all women have "horns" of jealousy, spite and other bad thoughts that should be concealed during the wedding ceremony.

In Zambia the fisherfolk who live on the shores of Lake Bangweulu get married in dugout canoes. The tribal chief, clad in robes of red and black, performs the ceremony from his canoe; the bride and groom attend in their canoes.

In Norway weddings are accompanied by feasting and many toasts. Here the groom offers his bride a drink of new beer, brewed specially for the occasion, from a carved, boatlike cup. She wears a traditional bejeweled antique crown.

To symbolize the bond of their marriage, the Hindu bride's sari is tightly knotted to her new husband's belt sash.

majority of Americans marry within the religious group—Catholic, Protestant, Jewish—they were born into. But religion is not a burning issue in America today and mutual tolerance is increasing; as a result, interfaith marriage increases every year.

The situation is comparable in other Western societies, although the actual frequency of intermarriage varies from group to group and from place to place. Where a group is especially large or cohesive, there is less intermarriage than where it is small or relatively disorganized. According to a 1955 study, the numerous Catholics of the U.S. Southwest, mostly speaking Spanish and following a way of life quite different from that of their Anglo-Saxon Protestant neighbors, have a low rate of intermarriage: only 8.7 per cent of Catholics in El Paso, Texas, marry outside their faith. In the Southeast, where there are relatively few Catholics and where there is little to differentiate their life from that of their neighbors, the rate is quite high: 70.3 per cent in Atlanta, for example. In Montreal, which has a large, homogeneous Jewish population, little marrying out of the faith occurs: just 5.6 per cent. But in the Canadian provinces of Saskatchewan and Alberta, where only a few Jews are scattered over an immense territory, the rate goes up to 34.8 per cent.

The rules of endogamy and exogamy are established by a society to govern marriages in a way that furthers the ends of the society itself. But the couple's parents also have their say; their interest is generally a family one. They want to make sure that their children find wives and husbands of whom the family can be proud. Indeed, both the family's good name and its fortune are at stake in every marriage. Sometimes marriage is an important step in moving a family up the social ladder, as when a rich but lower-caste Hindu girl can snare the younger son of a Brahmin family, or when the Duke of Marlborough deigns to take a plain Miss Vanderbilt as his bride. Sometimes marriage is a way of increasing wealth. "It's not that man marries maid," a German peasant once said, "but field marries field, vineyard marries vineyard, cattle marry cattle."

The marriage of field with field and of vineyard with vineyard may be contracted while the marrying partners are still in the womb as sometimes used to be done in China and Korea. A more usual custom is to marry off the children while they are still in their infancy, a practice that is now legally banned but nevertheless still followed in parts of India. In bygone days the royal houses of Europe were continually arranging marriages between toddling princes and princesses in the pursuit of dynastic aims, and noble and bourgeois families were quite ready to imitate them. Old church records are full of notations like this one from Chester, in England, recording the marriage of a three-year-old boy in the 16th Century: "He was hired for an apple bie his uncle to goe to the church." This is one old custom that has fallen into disuse.

But marriages for more than an apple remain the norm in most cultures. In these unions, more or less overt financial transactions may be involved, and sometimes they are the overriding consideration. Indeed, the

English word wedding comes from the Anglo-Saxon *wed*, meaning surety. The wed was a down payment in cattle, arms or money made by the prospective bridegroom to the family of his intended as a token "that he desire her in such wise that he will keep her according to God's law, as a husband shall a wife." In Murdock's *Ethnographic Atlas*, a collection of regional and cultural facts and statistics, more than two thirds of the societies listed insist on some handing over of valuables as part of the marriage process. "Valuables" may mean horses, as among the Cheyenne; pigs (the Ifugao society in the Philippines); dogs' teeth (Manus in the Admiralty Islands); bird-of-paradise plumes (Siane in New Guinea); brass rods (Tiv in Nigeria); or reindeer (Chukchee in Siberia). They may also take the form of a specified number of years' work: a Subanum bridegroom in the Philippines is required to work three to five years for his bride's family, and Jacob in the Bible had to work twice seven years so that he could marry his uncle Laban's two daughters. Among the Tiv, a man who is not rich in brass rods may give another man his sister in exchange for marrying the other fellow's sister.

Payments go in either direction, or in both. The man's family may pay

the better part of a century, Niagara
ls was known as the "Honeymoon
pital of the World." Newly wed couples
 this stylish group shown here in
3 converged on the scenic wonder by
n, and later by car, to stare first at the
s and then at each other. But in
 years after World War II the falls
an to go out of style as jet travel
le other resorts more fashionable.

a "brideprice" or supply "bridewealth," or the woman's family may provide a "dowry," or both may make contributions. The bridewealth or dowry goes sometimes to the family of the prospective partner, sometimes directly to the young couple. No convincing theory has yet been offered to explain why certain societies choose one of these alternatives rather than the other.

The importance given financial matters does not mean that marriage is a purely commercial transaction, that the young people are traded or bought outright like so many calves and heifers. The elders who arrange the wedding may be thinking primarily of the good of the family, but they are not insensitive to the needs and wishes of their offspring. To make a choice that is satisfactory on both counts, many societies call on the services of professional go-betweens and matchmakers like the *nakohdos* of Japan. Although the younger generation tends to look down on them as a relic of feudal days, the *nakohdos* were estimated to be arranging a good half of the marriages in Japan as late as 1960.

The art of matchmaking can be as complex and as formal as a traditional folk dance. Here is how a County Clare farmer described to anthropologist Conrad Arensberg the Irish practice of using relatives —called friends in the brogue—to handle the preliminaries: "The young man sends a 'speaker' to the young lady, and the speaker will sound a note to know what fortune she has, will she suit and will she marry this Shrove? She and her friends will inquire what kind of a man he is, is he nice and steady. And if he suits, they tell the speaker to go ahead and 'draw it down.' So then he arranges for them to meet in such a place on such a night, and we will see about it.

"The speaker goes with the young man and his father that night, and they meet the father of the girl and friends . . . The young lady's father asks the speaker what fortune does he want. He asks the place of how many cows, sheep and horses is it . . .

"Well, if it is a nice place, near the road, and the place of eight cows, they are sure to ask £350 fortune. Then the young lady's father offers £250. Then maybe the boy's father throws off £50. If the young lady's father still has £250 on it, the speaker divides . . . so now it's £275. Then the young man says he is not willing to marry without £300—but if she's a nice girl and a good housekeeper he'll think of it. So, there's another drink by the young man; and then another by the young lady's father, and so with every second drink till they're near drunk."

These are only the preliminaries. There may be many more consultations and visits, but if all goes well, papers are eventually signed, the girl's father hands over the money and the boy's father signs over the farm to the young people. The result is a fair enough deal all around. The bride's parents have ensured that she will be well provided for, with an adequate farm, and their standing in the community will not suffer as it would if they let her go to a place too far off the road. The groom's parents have received a "fortune" they can use for their own old age, but more

69

Packaged honeymoons in the Poconos

In America, where many a grandma and grandpa honeymooned sedately at Niagara Falls, their newly wed grandchildren have a more hedonistic option. They can revel at resorts offering luxurious kitsch for honeymoon couples.

The one shown here, Cove Haven in Pennsylvania's Pocono Mountains, offers a package deal to some 200 couples a week who find, as the brochure put it, "love's beginning." They may be distracted, however, by 49 activities, including a group hot-dog roast. After a full day, couples retreat to rooms with roaring fires and oversized beds. This resort is one of eight such havens in the Poconos, all within champagne squirting distance of one another.

Champagne at hand, a couple lolls in one of the honeymoon resort's heart-shaped sunken bathtubs. Another such retreat for newlyweds goes a step further: it offers the couple a small but private swimming pool right off the bedroom.

To while away the hours, newlyweds are offered numerous amusements and distractions. Among them are (clockwise from the top) round beds and fireplaces in the cottages, bathing in a heart-shaped swimming pool, horseback riding on tree-shaded trails as well as dancing in a discotheque. Love knows no season at Cove Haven. The resort roars along right through the winter months, with skiing and skating, tobogganing, snowmobiling, indoor bowling and swimming.

probably will use to furnish dowries enabling their own daughters to find suitable husbands.

This procedure seems centuries removed from the modern world of informal mingling. In most industrialized societies today, it is up to young people and not their parents to pop the question, fix the date and make arrangements for the future. In America, at least, such liberties have become traditional. As long ago as 1842 an Austrian visitor named Isidora Löwenstern commented: "A very remarkable custom in the United States gives girls the freedom to choose a husband according to their fancy; practice does not permit either the mother or the father to interfere in this important matter."

Löwenstern was perhaps overly impressed with surface indications. Admittedly, marital choice in the United States is free when judged by the standards of other cultures. But a close look at the situation in America —and elsewhere—shows that parents often have a considerable role in that choice even though they do not impose their will directly through infant marriages or through arranged alliances. Somewhere in the background the family is always lurking, pushing or nudging its children in the direction it wants them to go.

A subtle kind of influence is exercised when parents choose to live in a particular neighborhood where their daughter will be constantly thrown together, at school, parties, athletic events and the like, with boys of a particular social stratum. The idea, of course, is to increase her opportunities for an economically and socially advantageous marriage. As a matter of fact, the whole process of child rearing, looked at with the cold eye of the economist, can be seen as an effort to maximize the price a child will command on the marriage market by the time he comes of age. Parents make—and are proud of making—considerable sacrifices in order to achieve this end. They buy expensive homes in exclusive neighborhoods, send their children to expensive schools and camps, and buy them expensive automobiles, all with the purpose of gaining them entrée into a world where they will presumably find richer, more fashionable and altogether more desirable spouses. Add the teas, the socials, the debutante parties, the cotillions; add the shower of gifts that most families these days think it obligatory to let fall on young couples; add, if necessary, the psychiatrist's bill; and it becomes clear that the father of the bride or groom may spend thousands on preparing his darling for matrimony.

The launching of the new family must be ceremonial and public, only the details of the ceremony varying from class to class and from culture to culture. The Colonel's lady coming down the cathedral aisle with six bridesmaids holding her long train, and Judy O'Grady being married at an open-air hippie bash while the onlookers chant Hare Krishna, read poems by e. e. cummings, or perform exotic Indian dances, are sisters under the skin. So are all brides, whether they follow the rituals of Turkey, Japan, Norway or India.

These ceremonies perpetuate ancient traditions, but many of them include elements that are newer than is generally thought. Many people look on a wedding as an old religious rite whose forms are to be honored, or not, as piety dictates. Their view is an error of perspective. In only a minority of the world's cultures has religion played as important a role in marriage as it has in recent times. Ancient texts like the Bible and Homer speak often of marriage festivities, never of marriage liturgies. In St. John's account of Jesus' first miracle, at the wedding in Cana of Galilee, there is mention of a "ruler of the feast," but not of any priest. This omission may reflect the low regard in which marriage was held by early Christian leaders. St. Paul, a bachelor, wrote to the Corinthians: "I say to the unmarried and widows, it is good for them if they abide even as I. But if they cannot contain, let them marry for it is better to marry than to burn." Burn with the fires of lust, that is: marriage was to Paul a lesser evil that kept people from indulging in sex under circumstances that he considered less righteous.

Marriage remained a civil ceremony for almost the whole first millennium of Christianity's existence. It was only in the Ninth Century that a marriage liturgy was created, and even then the ceremony was not tolerated inside churches, where the ground was considered too holy for a rite with such carnal overtones. At first, a priest united couples on the porch in front of the church doors. Only after marriage had been accepted as a sacrament of the Church for some centuries was the service allowed to move indoors. Christians have not always been happy with that change. The 17th Century Puritans, who prided themselves on restoring the pristine purity of the early Christians, repudiated church weddings, and in the Massachusetts Bay Colony a clergyman was forbidden by law to officiate at a marriage even outside of church. Underlying this law was the Puritan view of marriage as a civil contract rather than a sacrament.

Today religion has declined in importance in many European weddings, while most American marriages take place in a church or synagogue, or at least with a clergyman in attendance. But in almost every aspect of the wedding, except for a few solemn ceremonial moments, commerce vies with religion in the United States, supporting a seven-billion-dollar marriage industry of wedding counselors, florists, decorators, caterers, band leaders, ballroom and hotel owners, dress designers, society editors, society photographers and specialized publications. Finally there are expensive, elaborate love nests and honeymoon resorts where the newly wed couples can get away by themselves, far from familiar prying eyes, to frolic to their hearts' content, free of all constraint.

All constraint, that is, but that of time. Like other moons, this one must wane. At the end of the period of carefree privacy, reminders that marriage is after and above all a social institution inevitably begin to come into focus. The hotel room in the honeymoon haven is only a flickering overture to a life of commuter trains, sinks full of dishes, crying babies and all the endless problems that go with raising a family.

Rosie Calvin waits in the basement of the church hall for her wedding to begin. Tables around her are set for the reception to follow.

The perils of teen-age marriage

When Rosemary Calvin and Bob Eck took their wedding vows in October of 1965, the cards may have seemed stacked against them. Each was only 18 years old, and the divorce rate among couples who marry in their teens is twice as high as that for the general population. And divorce statistics do not indicate all trials awaiting teen-age newlyweds. One survey found that 47 per cent of couples married in their teens said that they would not have married if they had to do it over again.

The reasons for the failure of so many teen-age marriages are obvious. The partners normally are immature, and their unrealistic expectations founder on the day-to-day frictions and drudgery of marriage.

But Rosie and Bob were different. Both were more mature than most 18-year-olds and both were better prepared for marriage by experience. Bob had grown up doing chores on his family's farm in Glen Carbon, Illinois. Rosie had done all the housework in her home from the time she was nine years old. As a result of shouldering such responsibilities, they came to their marriage with few illusions.

More important, perhaps, Rosie and Bob were an old-fashioned couple who believed deeply in the institution of marriage and were determined to make it work. How well it has worked can be seen from the intimate before-and-after photographs by Charles Harbutt here and on the following pages. He became Rosie's and Bob's friend when he was assigned to document their wedding for the TIME-LIFE BOOKS publication *The Young Americans* and he was welcomed back eight years later to see how they were making out.

PHOTOGRAPHED BY
CHARLES HARBUTT

Bob and Rosie cut the cake at their wedding reception—a hushed moment as they start their lives together, young lovers unaware of the problems ahead.

Becoming a family

From the start, Bob and Rosie had no illusions that marriage began and ended with the cutting of the wedding cake. Both were level-headed people, aware of the pitfalls, and determined not to take things at too fast a pace.

Looking back on those early years, they believe they owe much of the success of their marriage to the decision to wait awhile before having children. As Rosie says, "I think the biggest problem for most teen-age marriages is that young kids have kids right off the bat. I think they should have a chance to know each other first." Rosie and Bob spent the first few years doing just that.

When Bob was drafted into the Army in 1966, the couple went off to Germany together. "We had some nice times," Rosie remembers. "Nobody influenced us, and we really did grow together."

That growth helped to sustain them when they returned 18 months later to begin family life in earnest. Their first child, Robert, was born in October 1969, their second son, Richard, in 1971. By that time Bob was out of the Army, and Rosie was prepared to become a full-time mother.

Eight years later Rosie and Bob Eck are solid, mature couple in their own hor with two children. They have establish themselves in the world as a fami

Young and pensive, on the morning of his wedding Bob leaves behind his boyhood on the farm he loved. He still hopes someday to live on a farm of his own.

Head of the house

Both Rosie and Bob were determined to establish a traditional husband-wife relationship; Bob puts it in traditional terms: "The man is the head of the household, the breadwinner, the woman takes care of the home."

From the start, they worked and scrimped to make such an arrangement possible. After Bob got out of the U.S. Army, he studied pollution control and supported his growing family with three part-time jobs.

When the five-room house Bob and Rosie owned needed extensive repairs, Bob, a skilled craftsman, did the work himself. "He put all new windows in the house," Rosie recalls, "and I just thought they were going to fall out, and he put a furnace in just after we had Bobby, and I was sure that was going to blow up, but little by little I found out he was doing things right."

Bob felt he was doing things right, too. When he completed his college studies he won a job as a water inspector for the state of Missouri. Now he was not only the head of the household but a bona fide breadwinner as well.

In his office Bob catches up on some paperwork. He spends most of his time inspecting water systems around the county, but files reports from the office.

At home Bob emerges from his workshop to relax with the family for a minute. His skill at carpentry has always provided the Ecks with an extra source of income.

On the job after her honeymoon, Rosie feeds a patient while training as a practical nurse at St. Elizabeth's Hospital in Granite City, Illinois. She later trained to become a psychiatric nurse.

Homemaker

Rosie Eck is a creative, energetic woman whose perception and adaptability are major factors in the success of her marriage. She frankly admits that when first married she was the dominant partner. "I used to say jump, and Bob would first say how high, and then jump. It's just the opposite now."

Rosie worked as a psychiatric nurse at first, but then she became pregnant, and because Bob was the kind of old-fashioned farm boy who felt that his wife should be home taking care of the children, she gave up the job and turned her creative energies to motherhood. "I spend much of my day with the boys," she says. "When lunchtime comes we have a game. I'm the restaurant lady, and they're the firemen or the postmen. I'm mommy only when they fight."

Despite her concentration on her children, Rosie makes time for interests of her own. She had developed a flourishing business selling home-baked cakes to neighbors and friends and later expanded her efforts, setting up a booth for her cakes at a local fair and teaching a cake-decorating course.

Rosie squeezes star-shaped designs onto a birthday cake for her son Richard. A talented baker, she operates a small but successful dessert-making business at home, creating new designs for each cake.

A gentle disciplinarian, Rosie admonishes Richard, three, to keep his hands off the laundry she has just washed, while four-year-old Robert obediently starts to put on his pajamas in preparation for bed.

Rosie's and Bob's first fight as newlyweds erupted over the location of their bed. Bob wanted it in the middle of the room, Rosie against the wall. Rosie won.

Sources of conflict

Bob and Rosie started married life with a lively argument *(above)*. "We had some doozies the first year. The second year too!" Rosie recalls.

But both young people soon recognized the need for eliminating controversy, and they realized that there were two things they were going to have to do if their marriage was to survive. One was to share the burdens of housekeeping and child raising, and the other was to listen to each other carefully instead of shouting and screaming when a problem happened to come up.

Now, when Bob comes home at night, instead of stretching out to relax, he takes over the disciplining of the children, helps put them to bed and lends a hand with other chores. "I try not to take advantage of Rosie by pulling the too-tired routine," he says.

And when a conflict arises—whether it is the current high cost of groceries, the purchase of a new dress for Rosie or the price of a new sander for Bob's carpentry, the two hear each other out and arrive at a joint decision instead of having another doozie.

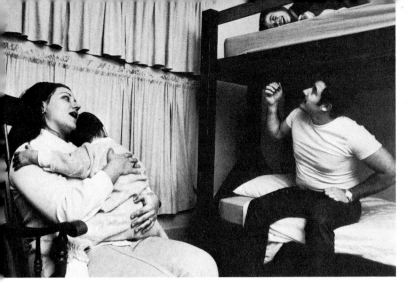

The Ecks share the task of putting
the children to bed. Bob is less inclined
than Rosie to put up with their classic
devices for postponing the final lights-out.

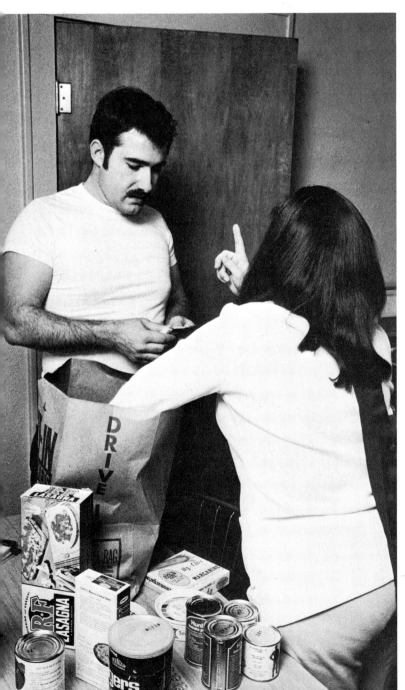

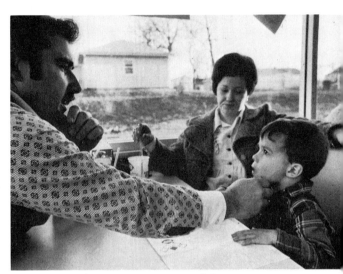

At a local restaurant, Rosie looks on while
Bob tells Richard to stop talking:
"Get on with eating your hamburger or
else we'll be here till seven o'clock."

In the kitchen Rosie explains where the
grocery money went. Bob sometimes
questions food expenditures, but he listens
carefully to Rosie's explanations.

Just married, Rosie hesitantly reaches out to touch Bob's face in a motel bedroom after their wedding in 1965. Because it was the first time that Bob had ever checked into a motel, he found himself wondering, "Do I give both names?"

Eight years later and still in love

None of the accommodations and compromises, and none of the growth that has occurred in Rosie's and Bob's marriage would have been possible except for the single enduring quality of old-fashioned love. The two have an unabashedly romantic feeling for each other, mingled with respect and trust.

Rosie finds everything that she wants in Bob. "He fulfills everything I never had," she says, and adds, "He's kind and he's considerate, any place, any time, and you could say that I adore him for the way he treats me."

Bob reciprocates. He appreciates Rosie as a "great mother," and he acknowledges that the time and affection that she has devoted to their two sons have been invaluable to their development as curious, lively, emotionally secure individuals. Beyond that, he appreciates what Rosie has meant to him. "She is there whenever I need her," he says. "She is always ready to console me if I have a problem. She is a fun person to be around, a very warm, outgoing person who is always willing to help. She's a super wife."

*Bob gives Rosie a Rudolph Valent[i]
embrace—as he does every day when
comes home. Rosie makes a consci[o]
effort to keep her husband what she ca
"interested." She says she sometin
"chases," sometimes plays "hard to ge[t]*

Dependents Old or Young

Pearl Buck, author of *The Good Earth,* had a dearly loved daughter, born during her mother's long residence in China, about whom she later wrote a book called *The Child Who Never Grew.* The girl was lovely and affectionate, but her mind stopped developing before she was four. One day Miss Buck was painfully reminded of the callous attitude of many people toward such children: on a Shanghai street, a well-dressed American tourist stopped to stare at the little girl and said, "The kid is nuts." When the Buck family moved back to the United States, their daughter became an impossible burden on her parents' lives and careers. After agonizing debate, they sent her to a boarding school for retarded children where, amid toys and kind teachers, she could live out the years that by conventional standards must be judged empty.

American friends agreed that residence at the school was best for the child as well as for her father and mother. But Miss Buck's numerous Chinese friends were shocked and incredulous. For in prerevolutionary China, such misfortunes as the birth of a handicapped child were understood and accepted as part of the divine plan. There were no institutions for the unfortunate; as a matter of course, families fitted their infirm elderly relatives and their crippled or defective children into their households as best they could. In the eyes of Miss Buck's Chinese friends, it was contrary to all order and decency to leave a child among strangers. Surely, they thought, there were grandmothers or aunts or unmarried cousins who would be glad to stay at home and take care of the little Buck girl. Surely this was a family matter and a family duty.

The tragic dilemma faced by Pearl Buck lies outside the experience of most families. So does the poignant awareness of cultural differences she must have felt when she decided to institutionalize her daughter. Nevertheless, her problem is a reminder that virtually every family has dependents of some sort. And her confrontation with clashing social values highlights the anthropological fact that families living in different societies characteristically choose different ways of caring for and relating to their dependents, both young and old *(left).* Seeking ways to sustain them, families have two options: to take on the task themselves, or to look for outside help. Their ultimate decision depends partly on the nature of the culture in which they live, on whether or not it is essentially modern in outlook, or more or less old-fashioned. And what they decide has important consequences for guardians and wards alike.

All families by their very nature are set up for dependency; the family institution exists primarily to care for children. But many families must also provide for additional types of dependents, and some of them are more dependent than others. Their dependency may be temporary, as when father or mother falls ill and has to put aside the role of breadwinner or housekeeper for a period of time; or it may be permanent, as in the case of Pearl Buck's child. It may result from an accident before birth or long afterward. But much more often it is a result of the eternal process in which all human beings begin life as helpless babes, while most end it as feeble, if not wholly decrepit, oldsters.

The traditional family fits the old and the young together into its way of life. It does so partly because there is no alternative; there is no one else to pick up the burden. Most societies today, as in the past, are too poor, or their social organization is too rudimentary, to provide institutional facilities for weaker members even though these dependents may be putting great strain on the resources of individual families. Caring for the weak is not only a matter of necessity, however. In many traditional family systems, a sense of loyalty to one's own kind is built in from the start. Kinsmen are expected to stick together and share alike. If one individual is weaker than the others, he may have less prestige than his fellows, but he is still included in the system of mutual protection and is entitled to all the care the family can afford to give.

The nuclear family that has evolved in the more advanced and affluent Western societies characteristically takes a different view of its responsibilities. The goal is generally the greatest comfort of each of its members, and it tries to find a course of action that is best for all concerned. It frequently calls in outside professional advice, and often is eager to abdicate its caretaking functions to outside authorities. Everybody goes out, or is taken out periodically, for treatment by doctors, dentists, orthodontists, psychiatrists and family consultants, and on their recommendation a family may pack off difficult or hopeless cases to institutions for periods ranging from a few hours to the remainder of a lifetime. In fact, the proliferation of kindergartens, day-care centers, hospitals, asylums and retirement homes is one of the characteristics that distinguishes modern Western society from all other societies past and present.

In such institutions efficient, bureaucratic care replaces, or is supposed to replace, the generally affectionate and well-intentioned but perhaps slapdash methods of relatives ministering to their kin in private dwellings. What the new method gains in efficiency, it may lose in the human warmth provided by an old-fashioned family in an old-fashioned home. Sometimes the gain is all to the good. Most people would agree that a well-staffed operating room is a better place to have an appendix out than the most comfortable bedroom at home. But there are many cases where the choice is not so clear-cut. The modern family is often faced with the necessity of weighing the different benefits of home and institutional care and making a choice that may be traumatic for the family either way and that may also have crucial, and unforeseeable, consequences for the future of the dependent person.

For instance, an apparently senile relative may be exceedingly difficult to cope with around the house, yet if he is institutionalized, his visiting family must expect to witness the painful spectacle of his still further deterioration. Recent research has suggested that if his family can tolerate him at home while seeing to it that he gets a more nourishing diet and more stimulating contacts with other people, there is at least a possibility that his senility will disappear. In one case, a retired financier of 70 became troublesome because of his paranoid suspicions and was at first diagnosed as a victim of organic brain disease. Nevertheless, instead of being consigned to a hospital, he was treated with psychotherapy and was helped to find a job as treasurer of a charitable organization. His symptoms of paranoia disappeared completely.

Similarly, a retarded child may be happier in the familiar family atmosphere and, as the center of everyone's attention and care, may develop abilities that would never appear in the impersonal atmosphere of an institution. An example is Allan Schenkein, a victim of the severe form of retardation called Down's syndrome or mongolism. Schenkein is a man of about 40 with an IQ less than 75. Lovingly nurtured at home by his parents, he has learned to travel alone by public bus to a simple job doing light factory work in a Denver agency for the retarded. Allan's father wrote, in a tribute to his son, "Allan astonished us with some creative writing" that was "not prose, not poetry," but always touchingly expressive. On one occasion, in his labored, childlike handwriting, Allan set down his feelings on a lovely day: "Summer in the West when everything is quiet and clear, with everything beautiful and green, with wild flowers of all colors, and a small water creek, and a beautiful blue sky. And the trees are very still. Sometimes a small breeze."

Raising and caring for such a retarded person may be a deeply rewarding experience, as it has been for Allan Schenkein's father, and it can be a factor in holding a family together more tightly. But a retarded child can also cause strain between parents, or between the parents and their other children. A normal child (in practice generally a sister) who spends prolonged periods helping to care for a retarded sibling may, according to research by Bernard Farber and his associates, be affected by the weight of such premature responsibilities. "The mother," they say, "whose daughter interacts frequently with the retarded child tends to view the daughter as moody, stubborn, easy to anger."

Retarded children are fortunately an uncommon burden. Not so the elderly. The form of infirmity with which the family most often must deal is that resulting from aging. Gradual loss of elasticity in body and mind, shrinking and wrinkling, atrophy of faculties, crankiness and failures of memory—these are universal consequences of advanced years, and every society has had to develop its own strategies and principles for dealing with its aged dependents.

In some instances the strategy may seem harsh or even cruel. Reverence for the old is not a biological instinct or even a universal human practice. Man's cousins the anthropoid apes, whose social life has given many hints to anthropologists speculating about primitive man, live in hordes in which the ranking male tyrannizes the younger ones, and as long as he is in good health, insists on a sexual monopoly of the attractive females. When his teeth begin to go, younger males take cruel revenge for the harsh treatment they have received from him: they drive him out to live in a solitude that ensures his early death by violence or undernourishment.

Some peoples living harsh lives in a difficult environment seem to have no more regard or affection for their old than do the apes. Beaten unmercifully in their youth, the Yakuts of Siberia beat their parents unmercifully when they are finally able to snatch control of the family herds of cattle and horses from the failing hands of their elders. "Why should I treat my mother kindly?" a Yakut asked a reproachful Russian visitor. "Let her cry! Let her starve! She used to begrudge me my food, she used to beat me any time she felt like it."

Other peoples abandon (or used to abandon) their old to die of exposure or starvation, though not necessarily with the harsh feelings of the Yakuts. One pathetic story tells of an Eskimo woman who has acceded to her aged father's wishes and pushed him into the icy ocean to drown. But he did not sink because of his bulky clothing. "Put your head down, Papa, it will be quicker," she cries to him with tears in her eyes. Such cases of abandonment have become rarer as contacts with a disapproving outside world have multiplied and as general living conditions have improved. In early days, Eskimos felt that they had no choice but to leave their enfeebled elderly behind. Like other groups living under severe climatic conditions—the Indians of the Bolivian jungles or of the Nevada deserts, for example—they had to keep moving all the time in search of rare and elusive game. If they had stopped every time grandfather faltered, the whole family might have starved to death.

Fortunately, nature does not require such harsh choices in most parts of the world. The general rule, followed or at least accepted in principle by almost every society more secure and more developed than the simple hunting communities of the Yakuts and the Eskimos, is that families take care of their own; children look after their parents when they are too weak to rule their own households. Fossils found at Shanidar in northern Iraq, where a nomadic people lived 100,000 years ago, suggest that the rule was already being observed in Neanderthal times. Among other bones, anthropologists found those of an old man who had been badly crippled, apparently from birth; one side of his body had evidently never developed properly, one arm had been severed just below the elbow and he had suffered from arthritis. It was plain that a person so handicapped could never

In France an experimental program helps the elderly avoid dependency by reinstating them in a traditional family role. As part of the program, this 72-year-old widow has been placed as a "grand'mère au pair," an adopted grandparent—she assists in caring for the children and helps with the housework in return for her room and her meals.

have survived had he been forced to fend entirely for himself in the harsh, pre-civilized world of the Neanderthals. This severely handicapped oldster must have been cared for, fed and protected by more vigorous and younger members of the tribe.

There are practical reasons for this protection afforded the elderly. In preliterate and preindustrial cultures, the physical weakness of the aged may make them a burden, for others may have to produce the food that nourishes them, but they have much to offer in return. They are not mere objects of charity; they are storehouses of practical knowledge untroubled by technological obsolescence. These societies are fairly static and expect to meet familiar problems in familiar ways. Length of experience is then an inestimable virtue. The old have spent uncounted years mastering the crafts—tiger skinning, blanket weaving and the like—on which prosperity depends. They are the ones who have learned by heart the ancient rites and incantations that protect against natural and supernatural malignancy. Their memory extends back to times of great and unexpected emergencies—a drought, perhaps, or a famine or an enemy invasion—and so they can draw on practical experience for sound advice when new emergencies arise. All the wisdom that in literate lands can be found in books is locked up in their heads.

Slowly and laboriously, Annie Mahaffey, 80, goes down a steep flight of stairs by herself. These two pictures were shot in 1959 for a LIFE magazine photo essay on the plight of the aged. A widow financially unable to support herself, Mrs. Mahaffey lived with her son's family, sharing the dependency status that is common to numerous elderly people.

Annie Mahaffey sits in the living room while the baby occupies her daughter-in-law and granddaughter. The old woman sometimes felt left out. "Because I'm eighty years old," she said, "nobody wants to listen to me. I have nobody to talk to."

Consequently these old people acquire considerable importance—sometimes even a preponderating influence—in their communities. Because of what they can do for the younger generation, they are revered as sages. It is no accident that seers, shamans, medicine men, magicians and holy men are generally of advanced years. Tiresias, the seer who correctly predicts doom in *Oedipus Tyrannus* and other plays by the great Greek dramatist Sophocles, was always presented as old to the point of decrepitude, and blind, his wisdom the product of long, sad experience in the world.

Often another kind of self-interest motivates the care of the old. Grown children look out for the welfare of their enfeebled parents because they want to set an example to their own children who, they hope, will look out for them someday. Sharon Curtin, the author of *Nobody Ever Died of Old Age*, cites the American folk tale—it has analogies in the Grimm brothers' collection of German tales and elsewhere—of the wooden bowl from which an elderly grandmother has to eat because her trembling hands might drop the valuable china one. When this explanation is given to her little granddaughter, the child says, "You must save the wooden bowl when Granny dies, Mummy." "What for?" asks the mother. "For when you are old," replies the little girl.

Beyond practical considerations, there are ethical reasons for taking care of aged people. In many places, respect is seen to be due the elderly even if they no longer make useful contributions to society. "There is no greater disgrace than to abandon the old," writes a student of an Arab village in Lebanon, and the same sentiment is echoed in anthropological descriptions of dozens of other communities the world over. The old are offered honorific titles. They are marched out on ceremonial occasions like state funerals or coronations. They are entitled to public recognition: "Thou shalt rise up before the hoary head," said God to Moses. In many cultures outward marks of respect are required, or at least considered good etiquette. Among the Bedouin, young men are expected to defer to the older generation at all times, and they are not permitted to mention women in the presence of the aged. Rajput women must cover their heads with their saris when an elder enters the room.

So much for what might be called the official view of old age in traditional families. There is, of course, another side to the picture; reality has frequently shown a disconcerting tendency to run counter to the finest ideals. Shakespeare's King Lear, howling on the heath at the ingratitude of his wicked daughters Goneril and Regan, bears witness to the truth that a prescribed reverence for age has not always prevented even the most "civilized" of children from neglecting, ruthlessly exploiting or maltreating their aged parents on occasion.

Writer Sharon Curtin, eloquently denouncing the modern world for a crudely mechanical and heartless treatment of the old, falls into sentimental distortion when she speaks of the aged in traditional families of the past, with their "quiet warm space by the fireplace to sit and watch your grandchildren play . . . cracker barrels to sit upon and speak of times past." The Wyoming country town where she grew up provided her with such happy visions, but it also included old people living abandoned to wretchedness and destitution, with no fireplaces or grandchildren or cracker barrels to their name.

The contemporary romanticizing about happy old age in the American past has been nurtured, without much doubt, by the fact that most records describe upper-class or at least relatively prosperous families; such pleasant visions do not take into account the majority of old people who were forced to live out declining years in grinding poverty unrelieved by Social Security, their perpetual aches unrelieved even by aspirin.

Even allowing for romantic illusions about golden years in the past, the fact remains that the family status of the aged has within a century or so undergone sharp transformation—and not always for the better. The importance the elderly had as custodians of wisdom in a static society is largely lost in a dynamic one characterized by constant technological and ideological change. What was once considered wisdom is now apt to look like old-fashioned foolishness. The old, anthropologist Margaret Mead has pointed out, are today the carriers of a dying culture, "a strangely isolated generation." Business and industry are constantly looking for new ideas, new methods, and in a sometimes illusory quest for efficiency they throw people out of jobs wholesale at ages when they are still capable of working. The family at home takes the same attitude: mother will turn to Dr. Spock for advice about how to care for baby rather than to the accumulated store of the grandmother's wisdom.

The obsolescence—real or imagined—of the older generation's knowledge is not the only difficulty. What makes the problem of the old ubiquitous is the fact that there are so many of them. Indeed it might be said that only recently has old age become a family problem, for the present is the first time the aged have made up a significant part of society. The old used to be a ragged band of survivors. In the days when life expectancy was in the thirties (as it was before 1800 in Europe and still is in many undeveloped countries), a 60-year-old was a rarity. Better diet, better medical treatment, better hygiene have changed all that. There were 20 million men and women over 65 in the United States in the early 1970s, 10 per cent of the total population, and the percentage rises steadily with each decade. The proportion is even greater in European countries: 12 per cent in West Germany, 13 per cent in France, 13 per cent in England and 15 per cent in East Germany.

The modern family thus is faced with a completely new situation. The father and mother are apt to come to the end of their working lives, with their children grown up and married and moved away, at a time when they are still in full command of their mental and physical faculties. They may be able to find new interests and activities to occupy them for the next few years, but what happens when their economic and physical resources begin to decline? Unlike the elderly Hopi, they cannot simply relinquish their sheepherding and gardening duties, move indoors, and weave blankets or baskets at home until they die.

For some fortunate few, a Hopi-like transition is possible. One example is the Lee family of Newtown, Connecticut. When the Lees' daughter Cindy was 16 years old, their household included not only Mrs. Lee's mother, Mrs. Edna Swinden, 75, but also her grandmother, Mrs. Harris Myers, 93. Running the house was a cooperative venture. Cindy and Mrs. Lee, a schoolteacher, did the shopping and cleaned the second floor, while the still-vigorous Mrs. Swinden did most of the ground-floor cleaning, all of the ironing and much of the cooking. Mrs. Myers made her own bed every day and took care of her personal needs. Assessing their unusual family, Cindy reported that she was sorry for youngsters who "only have their parents," and her father, a printing-plant executive, said he believed that when young and old live together, each gains a sense of history and of continuity. Things were not always idyllic, of course. "It gets rough at times," Mrs. Lee admitted. "But it's bound to when you have all these different personalities living together."

The Lees' accommodation to old-age dependency—on both sides, old and young—is a rarity, particularly in the United States. The aged seem to be more of a problem in America than they are in other wealthy countries for a variety of reasons, including a comparatively haphazard and inadequate system of social services, the geographic sprawl of a huge nation, and a tradition that seems to honor youth over age and individual independence over almost everything.

The startling fact is that only one fourth of all Americans over the age of 65 live with their families or friends—of the total of 20 million aged, 13.4 million maintain their own households. In 26 per cent of such cases, the elderly person lives by himself, perhaps miles distant from relatives. This independence may be largely a fiction, supported at high cost. Economic assistance from adult children is often essential. And then someone must look in—or at least telephone—every day (the nightmare of the responsible children is often verbalized: "What if Grandmother fell?"). Even the post-World War II suburban sprawl has had a powerful impact, posing new tasks for the adult children. Shopping centers, doctors' offices and churches are now scattered so far from residential areas and bus routes that they can be reached only by private automobile, and since many old people do not drive, they must be chauffeured even to accomplish something as simple and essential as buying groceries.

Many of these problems of the isolated elderly are being attacked. There are in some cities special buses for the aged, and schemes for delivering a daily hot meal to the home are being tested. Increased financial assistance provided by the Federal government has had a marked effect. The 1974 Federal Supplemental Security Income Program vastly broadened the coverage previously offered by Social Security, extending financial benefits to nearly double the number—6.3 million compared with 3.3 million—of aged, blind or disabled people. And the amounts of money paid these de-

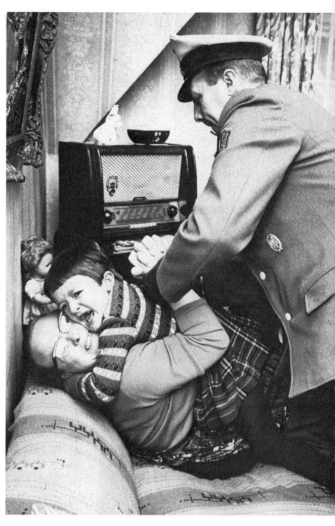

Society versus Christel Meyer

Children often are the victims of well-intentioned social forces that have a double edge. For society, while attempting to protect the rights of the individual, sometimes must act the villain.

A classic example revolved around a four-year-old German girl named Christel Meyer. Christel twice endured one of the most traumatic experiences that can befall a child—separation from her parents. Her mother died, and she came to love a foster mother. But then a court ruled that Christel belonged with her aunt and uncle, and police had her forcibly removed in the distressing and tearful scene recorded here.

The lasting harm caused by court-ordered custody struggles is difficult to predict. Outwardly, Christel Meyer accommodated happily to the situation, but the full extent of the psychological damage inflicted by the twice-enforced transfer may never be known.

Christel Meyer desperately resists transfer to her new guardians in this dramatic sequence photographed on the spot. She clutches her foster mother (left, above), then clings harder as a police officer intervenes. Finally wresting the weeping Christel free (right, above), the policeman prepares to remove the child — with the aid of the girl's new father — to her legal guardians' home (right).

pendents increased so that the government-provided income of many oldsters was well above the poverty level. In addition, many received supplementary income from state programs. Such actions lighten the burden of dependency and also alleviate the loneliness felt by the elderly who live by themselves. Governmental policy seems aimed to support their independent existence. The 1971 White House Conference on Aging does not even count "move in with a relative" as a category to consider in its report on housing the elderly.

The aged cherish their semi-independence. Among those who live apart from their families in retirement villages among other old people, one survey found that only 4 per cent said they missed their families. Such people may resist moving in with the children even after they need help in cleaning their quarters and preparing meals. They know, and the children know, that the addition of an elderly dependent can be disruptive. Modern homes are small, and while no real-life grandma is likely to be treated like the fictional one in Edward Albee's caustic sketch *The Sandbox* and sent to sleep under the kitchen stove, she may find herself sharing a room with baby. The aged are extras, often unable to participate fully in young family life, and often intolerant of its style. They are generally beloved, but perhaps resented. "If there are any conflicts in a family," comments Else Siegle of New York's Community Service Society, "they will get bigger when another adult moves in."

If the introduction of an aged dependent into the home sometimes provokes a family crisis, a more intense one generally attends an alternative (or subsequent) change in his dependency: his transfer to what used to be called the old folks' home and is now known as a nursing home. To some old people, such a move means they are being shipped off to die. Their view is distressingly correct in many cases, for a substantial proportion of the nursing homes provide only minimal care, and institutionalized routine can speed mental deterioration. Yet for someone who has no family to look after him, or who needs constant, expert tending, care in such a facility may be essential.

In the early 1970s, about 7 per cent of elderly Americans were confined to institutions of one kind or another, while in England and Wales the figure was 5.6 per cent. In France and West Germany the figure was under 3 per cent, but that may be partly because there are fewer old age and nursing homes in those two countries. Even in Japan, where family ties are traditionally very close, there was increasing reliance on nursing homes, and there were hints of a similar trend in China. Noting that the Chinese Communists have put out a pamphlet urging young people to take care of the elderly, Harvard psychoanalyst Martin Berezin remarked that "If they wanted to do it, they wouldn't have to be exhorted."

Moving a beloved old person into a nursing home severely increases the burden of his dependency on his family. The emotional stress on those who must make the decision is so severe that the change is often delayed too long. And the financial shock may be overwhelming. In America, government assistance is limited. Admission to public institutions is difficult to get and may require humiliating machinations, often of doubtful legality, to meet means tests. If a private nursing home must be used, the cost is shocking; paying the bills for one aged parent would require the major part of a responsible child's income—one half or more of a schoolteacher's salary, for example. To many middle-class Americans, it seems that only the rich can afford to grow old.

If the dependency of the aged is likely to bring pain and guilt to the family, that of children, by contrast, generally brings hope and joy. For it is through children that parents carry their joint creation, the family, into the future. On the purely material level, they may depend on their children for support and sustenance in the future; whatever they spend on them today is sometimes a form of investment they expect will be paid back, perhaps many times over, before they die. But so long as the children are children, they remain dependents, and their dependency to a great extent sets the course of the family.

The arrival of the first baby in a family announces a major change, sometimes an upheaval, that alters the lives of a man and woman even more profoundly than their marriage. The scope of this upheaval has been explained by James Bossard and Eleanor Boll, professors of child development at the University of Pennsylvania. "The coming of a child," they observe, "is like the advent of a new sun or planet into the solar system. The center of family life shifts. . . . Everything in the home comes to be viewed in relation to the children."

Sometimes the main effect of the child's arrival is a new closeness between husband and wife; sometimes it is irreconcilable conflict. For the marriage partners must now adapt themselves to entirely new roles: instead of merely functioning as husband and wife, they must learn how to play the part of father and mother, and many couples are simply unable to make the adjustment. Sociologist Robert Williamson wrote, "Often the strain of parenthood is a principal cause of disengagement and disenchantment," and sociologist Ira Reiss, summarizing the results of several studies, concluded in 1971 that while most couples report some decline over the years in the pleasures of marriage, the drop is greatest for couples with children. The strain is likely to be most pronounced during the early months of parenthood. When sociologist E. E. LeMasters conducted a 1957 study of 46 married couples, 38 of them told him that the arrival of their first child had touched off a serious crisis.

For most young parents the roles of father and mother are not only new but surprisingly difficult. Dr. Benjamin Spock is not exaggerating when he writes that "child rearing is a long, hard job." For both parents there may be sleepless nights during the baby's first weeks, when the child demands to be fed at short intervals and may wake up at odd hours screaming in protest over a wet diaper, an open safety pin or some mysterious discomfort that the new mother and father may not succeed in understanding or as-

suaging, however hard they try. For the mother, there is an endless round of baby care superimposed on normal household tasks, almost constant confinement at home and, especially if she has had to give up a good job, anger at being suddenly deprived of adult companionship. As the first baby grows up and other children arrive, the needs of the younger generation may begin to seem insatiable. Their clamor for time and attention appears endless; they must be shepherded to the doctor's office, to the dentist's, to school, to scout meetings and sporting events, and to music lessons and to parties. "What did we do with our time before the children came?" many exhausted parents ask themselves.

There are innumerable curbs on parental freedom. If the family is cramped for living space, the choice of a new house may be determined less by price, personal taste or convenience to shops and jobs than by the nearness of playgrounds and the quality of schools. There may be financial pressures that require the family breadwinner to look for a second job or to rethink long-term career plans, perhaps switching to uncongenial but better-paying work so he will have enough money to feed, clothe, entertain and educate his offspring. Even then, the costs of child rearing may be so great that parents can no longer afford to pursue old hobbies or take up new ones. Vacations in distant places, requiring air travel, become all but impossible when plane fare includes not just two tickets, for the husband and wife, but three more for the children. Recreations in which the whole family can participate displace the father's golf games. The mother hesitates to invite people in for dinner knowing she must also get the children's supper and go through the time-consuming rituals of bedtime. In short, constrained by the particular needs of their offspring or by limits to their own time, energy and money, parents may often find themselves lamenting —guiltily—pleasures they could enjoy "if it weren't for the children."

These days, most behavioral scientists believe that parents need not feel guilty for experiencing—and gratifying—needs of their own. Sociologist Ruth Cavan of Rockford College observes that the "child-centered family," for which middle-class America has become especially well known, is in the process of giving way to the "person-centered family." In the former, the needs and wishes of the youngest generation were unthinkingly given priority; in the latter, adults as well as children are seen as being entitled to personal fulfillment. "Too much self-sacrificing is not good for parents or child," Dr. Spock holds, and psychiatrist Theodore Lidz concurs. Parents, he says, must be satisfied themselves if they are to have anything to give to their children, and the parents' happiness, both as individuals and as a couple, "is just as important as anything they may be able to do for a child or that they can give him."

A balance between the needs of children and the rights of adults is harder for parents to achieve than for experts to write about. Even more difficult, especially in an age of rapidly changing values, are the decisions parents must make about how to bring up children. This aspect of parenthood has become more perplexing with what Ruth Cavan describes as the change "from an authoritarian to a developmental conception of child rearing." Not so many years ago, says Cavan, parents were likely to see themselves as authoritarian figures who issued orders, commanded unquestioning obedience and taught all of their children the same set of inflexible rules for living. Nowadays, mothers and fathers are more likely to consider themselves benevolent guides and counselors who look on each child as a unique individual and try to foster the free development of his special personality so that he can decide for himself how to live and what kind of person he wants to be.

The parental responsibilities that begin with the birth of the first baby do not end until childhood is over. Just when that turning point comes varies from culture to culture and from one historical period to another. In some traditional forms of the extended family and in at least some senses, it may never come. The old countryman running his farm in rural Ireland, like his counterparts in many conservative rural societies, may be surrounded by a covey of "boys" who are his sons, 50 and more years old, working at his beck and call. Despite their gray hairs they are, to all practical intents and purposes, dependent children.

Such prolonged, even if only partial, dependency is of course the exception. For most cultures, a safe rule of thumb is that the end of childhood comes when a child begins to contribute economically to his family by full-time work, or leaves it entirely to lead an independent life elsewhere. The majority of the world's population is and always has been desperately poor, and it follows that the children of the poor become, and have always become, productive members of the community at a very early age. In a study called *The Family in Cross-Cultural Perspective*, William Stephens reports that nearly all of the societies described by ethnographers put children to work before they turn 10. "Typically," he says, "work begins somewhere between the ages of three and six, the load of duties and responsibilities is gradually increased, and sometime between the ages of nine and fifteen the child becomes—occupationally speaking—a fully functioning adult."

Here is another anthropologist telling how the Chukchee of Siberia "send boys of 10, and girls hardly much older than that, to help in tending the herd. I remember having met one summertime two such young reindeer-breeders, a boy and a girl. . . . They were walking through the bushes quite alone, staff in hand, and wallet on back. They had to walk some ten miles before they could reach their herd."

Until comparatively modern times, the Western world had a similarly pragmatic attitude toward childhood. The family's chief concern with its offspring was to get them out into the world, to turn them from economic liabilities into economic assets. The very notion of a distinct and uniquely valuable world of childhood, taken for granted today, was quite foreign to the outlook of the Middle Ages. In those days painters used to represent children as scaled-down adults with grown-up features; along with everyone else, artists were simply incapable of seeing childhood as anything

continued on page 107

In the one-room Cachihuango house, where the family weaving business is conducted, Alfonso spins while his brother holds a spindle. His mother and sister-in-law, kneeling in front of the loom, peel potatoes for the midday meal.

PHOTOGRAPHED BY
BERNARD WOLF

The child as breadwinner

Dependency is a two-way street. Children depend on their families for care, but many families also rely on their children for economic assistance.

In the United States today, children under 16 make up a fourth of the farm work force during peak seasons, and some schools in rural areas close briefly to release them to the fields.

In many parts of the world, school is a luxury because the family's survival depends on the labor of the children from an early age.

Thirteen-year-old Alfonso Ramos Cachihuango, who lives with his family in the mountain village of Agato in Ecuador, works dawn to dusk to help support his family. The six dollars a week the Cachihuangos receive for weaving two *chalinas*, or shawls, saves

them from grinding poverty. Alfonso is an essential cog in the weaving business, and because his elder sister and brothers all have married and moved away, he is being groomed to take over when his mother and father have grown too old to work.

When he is not weaving, Alfonso works on the family's farm. He gets up at five in the morning, spends two thirds of the day weaving. The rest of the time he does farm chores and then sleeps in a lean-to in a field with his seven-year-old nephew Antonio.

This rigorous schedule may seem a hard life for a 13-year-old, but Alfonso's father has a ready explanation. "I don't want him to become lazy," he says. "Life is hard work and money is hard to come by. Alfonso must work."

103

Alfonso's father grinds some "tocti" berries for use in the dye that produces the characteristic reddish-brow color of the six-foot-long "chalina."

One of Alfonso's chores is to help his mother as she spins the carded wool into thread. To keep the puffy coil taut, she holds it wrapped around her arm.

Alfonso weighs the wool on a crude wooden balance. If he makes a mistake, the amount of wool that is processed may not be enough for a "chalina."

Bringing up a new boss

Everyone in the Cachihuango family has his own responsibility in the process of weaving *chalinas*. In addition to watching and helping his parents, and learning by observation, Alfonso is solely responsible for certain crucial steps in the process.

After the family has shredded the raw wool—a task that can take up to two days—Alfonso's first important job is to weigh the wool correctly. Then his mother cards and spins it.

But his main duty, under the watchful eye of his father, is the actual weaving of the two *chalinas* each week. He chooses the colors for the threads and then he carefully weaves them together on the loom.

After the weaving is done, Alfonso accompanies his mother and father to the market, and gravely watches as the *chalinas* are sold. One day, the whole responsibility will be his.

As his father separates the threads, Alfonso continues weaving a "chalina," a task that takes him about a day on the Spanish loom used by the villagers.

His lower lip jutting forward, Alfonso concentrates on the loom before him. Already, at the age of 13, he is doing a job traditionally performed by a man.

Alfonso watches carefully in the market at the end of the week. Here he learns the nuances of bargaining as his father negotiates with a potential customer.

else than a rather annoying, time-wasting preparatory stage for the important business of life. At about seven, children were thrown brusquely into adult life. Some of the poor went to work in the fields, while others were bound as apprentices to local craftsmen or to serve in rich men's houses. Upper-class boys began to learn riding and fencing almost as soon as they could walk, in preparation for their future careers as cavalry officers. Upper-class girls were expected to know how to run a house with a staff of servants by the time they were 10, and all were expected to learn the arts of life by living in the midst of it, among grownups.

In the past few generations the general level of well-being has risen enormously, skills have become more and more specialized and thus harder to learn, and humanitarian feelings against the exploitation of the weak have become almost universal. All these factors have worked to decrease and in some places eliminate the use of child labor. Beginning with the upper classes at the time of the Renaissance, and spreading gradually downward in succeeding centuries through the social scale, the custom has arisen of keeping children segregated from adult life. Everyone is supposed to go to school. In Europe, the educational process—and hence the period of a child's economic dependency—typically stretches out through the 15th or 16th year, and it lasts even longer for those young people who may be destined for careers in the professions.

In the United States, the establishment of free public schools and free "land-grant" colleges in 1863 meant that more and more youngsters began going to school for longer and longer periods. Nowadays only oppressed minorities like migrant agricultural workers, and a few fundamentalist religious sects like the Amish, follow the tradition of putting children to work in their early teens, although children from other groups may make token contributions to the family economy by holding part-time jobs. The great mass of children in Western society remain largely dependent on their parents for food, clothing, shelter, automobiles and everything else until they are in their late teens or early twenties. Those getting highly specialized training—to become physicians or research scholars, for instance—may continue to be dependent into their thirties.

The dependency of older children is often more trying for parents than that of younger ones, perhaps because the physical and mental maturity of these nearly grown-up youngsters accentuates the paradox of their dependency and magnifies the problems of the generation gap. Year by year the mass of dependent youth has been growing in size and power, until it has come to constitute a whole new social group, an entire new subculture. Because of its numbers, and because of the allowances that are freely or grudgingly given by parents, this subculture of the young deals from a position of great strength.

The youth subculture has enormous buying power, dictating fads and fashions and supporting entire industries. It feels its own importance; it makes itself felt in ways that drive its elders to fury or despair. It has its own codes of conduct, its own life styles, its own language. Watching their offspring smoking pot or swooning at rock concerts, parents may well be tempted to think that the end of all things is at hand. They are likely to be sure when young people "drop out," scorning the traditional work ethic to live in self-imposed indolent poverty, or when they live in coed college dorms and bring home opposite-sex friends on weekends expecting to share the same bedroom with them. Understating things somewhat, sociologist Robert Winch remarks that "This is one helluva time to be a parent."

It can be argued, however, that there is nothing new in the generation gap and that middle-class, city-dwelling parents of today are closer in outlook to their offspring than their own parents were to conservative rural grandparents. The lessening of conflict between generations is particularly noticeable in the United States, where millions of European immigrants saw their children growing up in the New World in ways completely foreign to their experience and often far beyond their powers to understand. The codes of conduct brought by parents from the villages of Sicily or Galicia were far different from those their children were to learn on the streets of New York or Boston or Chicago; memoirs of immigrants' children are full of cries of rage from the old and of equally loud cries of impatience from the young.

In a well-known essay, Arnold Green writes about the families of the Polish millworkers who lived in the Massachusetts town where he grew up. The old people had been raised in a tightly confined rural world, ruled by rigid tradition and convention, with every year and every generation following faithfully the pattern of the one before it. The young ones grew up speaking another language and mingling with other nationality groups in the open society of America with its tradition of continuous change. The result was a generation gap with a vengeance.

"As bewildered parents attempt to enforce old-world standards," Green writes of his hometown residents, "they are met with the anger and ridicule of their children. In answer to this, the parents have final recourse to . . . vengeful, personal, irrational authority. . . . In exasperation and fear of losing all control over their Americanized youngsters, parents apply the fist and whip rather indiscriminately. The sounds of blows, screams, howls, vexatious wails of torment and hatred are so commonplace along the rows of dilapidated mill-houses that the passerby pays them scant attention." The children fight back by maintaining a united front; they develop contempt for their parents, regarding them as "obstacles to be avoided, or circumvented wherever possible."

This, of course, does not sound like an ideal way to bring up children. But Green argues that for all their faults many of these Polish families achieved a kind of rough-and-ready stability. They held together despite the howls of which he writes, and their children by and large did not crack under the strain: none of the boys from Green's town was rejected by the army for psychoneurotic reasons in World War II.

In fact, it may well be that these boys would have survived less handily had they not rebelled against their parents. Although many observers see in the upsurge of the adolescent subculture a harbinger of the breakdown of nuclear families, if not of society as a whole, others take a more optimistic view. Sociologist Talcott Parsons, for example, maintains that youth's independence is its best guarantee of acquiring the abilities needed to face a changing and uncertain world.

In any case, each generation is apt to exaggerate the revolt of its own children. In the 1960s it was fashionable for college students to say that you can't trust any one over 30. As those who said it entered their thirties, it would seem that most of them became much like their parents. Certainly their successors on the campuses were less actively radical.

Some additional comfort for those who would like to be optimists may be found in Bronislaw Malinowski's description of the adolescent subculture on the Trobriand Islands. Like Americans, the Trobrianders were an affluent society, having—in the days before they acquired tastes for soda pop and transistor radios—a fairly easy living to be got out of jungle yam patches and the teeming sea. They too had no need of child labor: if adolescents wanted to go along on an adult hunting or fishing expedition for the fun and glory of it, that was all right, but they could drop out if they got tired. As a result of this attitude, Trobriand children too formed an autonomous body in their society, a little republic of their own that Malinowski describes as acting "very much as its own members determine, standing often in a sort of collective opposition to its elders." Adolescents led "a happy, free, arcadian existence, devoted to amusement and the pursuit of pleasure," indulging freely in love affairs that served to broaden their horizons: "Both sexes arrange picnics and excursions, and thus their indulgence in intercourse becomes associated with an enjoyment of novel experiences and fine scenery."

Western parents who frequently grumble that their children have no interest in them except to ask for money, borrow the keys to the family car or raid the icebox late at night, might find some comfort in the Trobriand experience: Parents there, Malinowski reported, were very much pleased with the way their adolescent children behaved and the Trobriand adolescents eventually settled down to stable family life like that of their fathers and mothers before them.

Stresses and Strains

The Greek myth of Antigone, handed down in the tragedy of Sophocles, depicts a recurring crisis in the life of the family: a challenge by forces outside itself. Antigone is a princess of the royal house of Thebes, but her brother Polynices has been killed making war against his native city. Their uncle Creon, ruler of the city, decrees that Polynices' body is not to be buried; it must be left on the field of battle to be devoured by beasts, the most degrading, to the Greek mind, of all punishments. Creon's position is simple: treason is the worst of crimes and must receive the most severe of retributions. Antigone reacts by taking a position equally simple: her duty to her family comes before any that she owes to Thebes. She buries the body, and Creon condemns her in turn to die.

Readers of the play give all their sympathy to Antigone, for Sophocles has concentrated on her solitary heroism in the face of heartless authoritarian law. But Creon has a good case to be made for him, and when people meet a Creon in real life they are apt to accede rather readily to his wishes. Usually he comes not in the guise of a bloody tyrant, but in that of some other external authority, such as the decent personnel officer of a giant corporation. If he announces to employees that the firm is moving to a distant city, he decrees the uprooting of routines and of friendships, changes of school for the children and of churches and social clubs for all. The move may impose a terrible strain on family life, yet statistics prove that most of the company's workers will move just the same. They value their families, but their families fit into a whole pattern of other institutions that may have overriding claims to loyalty.

Around the globe, relatively few families are asked to face the upheaval of moving so that the household head can keep a particular job. But no family anywhere, not even the most fortunate, is immune from stresses of some kind. They may come from without, as the church, the state, the schools or friends infringe upon the family's authority or external events challenge it. They may come from within, as illness strikes or individual members try to satisfy personal needs that may conflict with those of other members. These outer and inner pressures may ultimately strengthen family bonds, but their immediate effects are always disturbing; under stress, the happiest of families is sometimes unhappy. And in some cases, the clash of society and family, or of person with person inside a family, is so great that family cohesiveness is seriously threatened or even destroyed.

The external stresses on the family have emerged out of necessity. When society begins to develop beyond a primitive level, its members soon find that many tasks are better performed by agencies other than the family. Priests take over the job of interceding with the supernatural; police forces, armies and fire brigades take over that of protecting the family from physical harm; schools undertake to educate the children. And, in the complex modern world, the family often has little voice in what kind of work its members perform, or where, or for how long; all these matters are decided by the impersonal forces of the marketplace or by distant corporations, unions or government bureaus.

At the same time, these outside institutions, religious or governmental or private, frequently develop an identity and purpose of their own quite apart from their original function of serving or supplementing the family, and their special institutional needs may come to conflict with those of the family. For the family does not always find outside institutions helpful, and it never takes kindly to what it sees as encroachments on its authority. Old privileges may be jealously guarded, and their loss may be seen by the family as a sign that society is collapsing. Today, for example, the passionate battles of some American parents against sex education in the schools are but the latest in a long series of rear-guard actions against the constant expansion of outside power over a domain that once belonged entirely to the family. Indeed, much of world history can be seen as a record of the supplanting of autonomous family traditions by impersonal laws and institutions that often impose stress on the family.

When a new religion like Christianity bursts upon the world, it may bring a violent wrenching of old family ties. "If any man come to me," said Jesus (Luke XIV: 26) "and hate not his father, and mother, and wife and children, and brothers and sisters, yea, and his own life also, he cannot be my disciple." The early Christians were a missionary sect, and every time they made a convert, they stirred up strife with the convert's family, Jewish or pagan. Married Christians were expected to lead exemplary family lives and bring up their children in an atmosphere of devotion. But it was considered better to remain virginal and not marry or produce children at all; early Christians, feverishly looking forward to an imminent second coming and the end of the world, regarded family life as at best a distraction on the road to salvation. It was more important to hear the good news of the New Testament than to hold to old ties of the flesh. "Great is the reward for forgetting a parent," wrote St. Jerome, and his words are echoed by preachers of evangelical sects today.

When Christianity was no longer a persecuted minority faith and the church had become an official institution in which membership was compulsory for practically the whole population, the attitude toward the family changed. For at least a thousand years now, the Christian church and the family have been so closely intertwined that it is something of a shock to realize that it was not always so. The family serves the church by providing it with a continuing stream of souls to live under church laws and sacraments. The church in turn gives the family a code of morals and invests it with a touch of holiness that helps keep it stable. "The family that prays together stays together," runs a popular slogan, and statistics bear this out: divorce is less common when both parents are active communicants of the same church. Nevertheless, in a world of rapidly changing moral values, church attitudes toward such issues as birth control, abortion, adultery and divorce still occasion family stress.

Even more than religion, the state is a potential—and often an actual—cause of family strain, for in the modern world the state impinges on the family in almost every aspect of life. It may dictate where the family may or may not live. It may influence family work and spending patterns by setting minimum wages, by forbidding certain kinds of work like child labor, by favoring certain professions or industries through subsidies or tax advantages. It may try to control sexual behavior by prohibiting or limiting abortion, by forbidding interracial or intercaste marriages, by making divorce more or less difficult. It may try to control the number of offspring by encouraging or discouraging birth control, by taxing bachelors and childless families more than others, in some cases by paying cash allowances for children. It may try to ensure the smooth passage of property from generation to generation by uniform inheritance laws, or it may use inheritance taxes to prevent the accumulation of large family fortunes. Such measures curb family freedom, but they are not intended to destroy it. For the state needs the family to maintain internal peace as much as the family needs the state to protect it from outer foes. A stable family produces adults who can be counted on to obey community laws and customs, and to be good workers, soldiers or taxpayers as the state may dictate.

The state has long preempted a family role in determining what Johnny is to read and think and believe, and for this purpose it has created an institution called the school. The teachers in the schools generally tell their pupils they should obey their papas and mamas. But what teachers teach may be quite subversive of family patterns and may lead directly to disobedience and revolt. Such teaching is especially common when the school becomes an instrument of upward mobility, instructing children in techniques for getting on in a world their parents were never equipped to cope with. Lower-class children brought up above the station of their parents can make lives miserable for their families, as did Pip in Dickens' *Great Expectations,* by their snobbish pretensions and their contempt for the "uncouthness" of their own backgrounds.

It is not only through formal institutions like the state and its schools that the outer world brings pressures to bear on family members. There is also that amorphous mass known to sociologists as the peer group, meaning associates of similar age, class and general standing. They are the people with whom a person usually works, plays and relaxes. They are a source of satisfaction and comfort, but they may well be disruptive. Just

how disruptive they can be is well known to any wife who complains that her husband stays up to all hours drinking and gambling with his peers; to any husband who blames a bad dinner on the interminable *Kaffeeklatsch* to which his spouse seems to devote her waking hours; and to any parents who are shocked to hear little Johnny come home using words he surely never heard on Mummy's or Daddy's lips.

At the same time, the peer group answers a vital need by performing functions the family itself cannot fulfill. A particularly dramatic example of this need is provided by that common case of the household lacking a father. That the absence of a father has an adverse effect on boys is an idea widely accepted; there is no grown male at home on whom the boys can model themselves, and they become confused about their own roles in life. Research among American families in World War II and among Norwegian families where the fathers were away for long periods on whaling voyages indicates that children from fatherless homes are, at least for a while, more submissive, dependent and effeminate than those whose families are whole. Some studies, particularly in the black ghettos of the United States, suggest that these problems may sometimes be avoided if the missing authority is provided by a peer group.

The troubles of black youths in United States ghettos have been blamed on their matriarchal families; in many of their homes, life gravitates around the mother or grandmother. The legal father, if he exists, does not put in a regular appearance, or if he does, may be able to offer only limited financial or psychological support. The male children, according to some authorities, consequently acquire little idea of what they are supposed to do as men. They are riddled with doubts and insecurities, and they become "frightened and confused little boys."

But the Swedish scholar Ulf Hannerz, who spent two years living in and observing a ghetto in Washington, D.C., cast some doubts on such conclusions. Hannerz, who recorded his experiences in a remarkable book called *Soulside*, became skeptical of the reports when he compared them with the actual life of the streets through which he walked daily. Instead of "frightened and confused little boys" he saw bright, independent and self-confident ones. The reason for the boys' strength of character, he came to believe, was the absence not only of a father figure but of any adult authority, male or female. There were no grownups in their everyday lives. They were offstage somewhere, at home or at work, and the kids were on their own, sharing to the full in the jostling, rough-and-ready life of the streets. Their attitudes and their language, their manner of dress and posture, their whole way of living, were being shaped by their peer group. It, more than parents, was seeing to their upbringing and doing so successfully, at least in Hannerz's view.

Western culture looks down on such a way of life today. Psychologist Urie Bronfenbrenner, for one, argues that "children should not grow up associating only with other children because they haven't much to give each other." He explains that social values do not arise spontaneously in youngsters' breasts: they must be learned from older people who cherish these values and want to hand them down to their offspring. "If children have contact only with their own age-mates," asserts Bronfenbrenner, "there is no possibility for learning culturally established patterns of cooperation and mutual concern."

Yet the adult models Bronfenbrenner favors may be a late and special development in human society. The French writer Philippe Aries, whose *Centuries of Childhood* proposes a controversial new interpretation of the family, suggests that the peer-group influence observed by Hannerz may be more important. It is possible to maintain that the rowdy and apparently disorganized ghetto street life is in the mainstream of human experience, while the primly supervised life of the traditional Western family is an atypical if not deviant form of behavior. Aries demonstrates that up until comparatively recently most people spent as little time as possible in their homes, which were generally dark, damp and verminous. Social life was lived outside, in the marketplaces and village squares, noisily, indiscriminately, everyone rubbing elbows with everyone else—the sort of life that still goes on in the old Arab towns of the Middle East.

It was only gradually that the family, with increasing comforts at home and new standards of civility, began to wall itself away from the colorful life outdoors. Residential quarters became segregated by class, so that the rich could avoid the noise and smell of the poor. People could no longer barge into other people's homes at any hour and expect to be received cordially. The all-purpose room of the past, which changed its nature depending on the furniture moved into it, became differentiated into bedroom, dining room, living room and so on. Home, in short, was becoming a private place for the family, and as it did so family relationships began to warm up. Husbands and wives, parents and children, lived in closer contact. As the family relinquished more and more of its external functions, like defense and health care, to outside institutions, it strengthened its internal bonds. In the last few generations the process has speeded up dramatically. Increasing affluence has meant that even relatively poor families can live, splendidly isolated, in separate houses or apartments, their members spending more and more time interacting among themselves.

Yet no matter how tightly the family draws in on itself, the outer world cannot be kept out. It follows the family into the home. Television, radio, books, magazines and newspapers now subject adults and children alike to a flood of external ideas. Most of this broadening of outlook improves the quality of life; it has made people better informed and more sophisticated than ever before. But this great benefit is not achieved without cost. For the mass media's flood of information also transmits the stresses and conflicting attitudes of the outer world into the heart and mind of the family, challenging and often upsetting accepted values.

A classic description of this disruptive effect of the mass media on the family was written a long time ago by French novelist Gustave Flaubert in *Madame Bovary*. He related the story of a country girl who wrecked her

The same bouffant hairdo and made-up eyes bolster these New Jersey schoolgirls' sense of identification with their peers. Allegiance to such an outside group can conflict with family authority, as it did in this case—the girls' apprehensive glances are guilty indications that they have risked parental disapproval to keep a date they made with some boys.

own and her family's life by trying to act out the romantic poses of novels that she had read in school.

Today, the impact of the media, especially television, is much more immediate and pervasive. About 95 per cent of all American households had TV sets in 1972, and the figures for the other countries were comparable —96 per cent in Japan, for example. One of its most striking effects is the introduction into the home's normally peaceful environment of graphic scenes of violence. Through the medium of television, actual battles, assassinations, kidnapings, police actions and riots—to say nothing of fictional dramas including even bloodier scenes—are projected into the family living room. Research on children who are exposed to this on-screen violence indicates that it has an adverse effect on their behavior. One study, by Stanford University psychologist Albert Bandura, found that children who watched TV violence behaved afterward twice as aggressively as youngsters who had not been exposed to such images. Urie Bronfenbrenner foresees that endless hours of watching violent TV shows will produce "increased alienation, indifference, antagonism and violence on the part of the younger generation in all segments of our society."

Yet for some people TV may serve as a pacifier rather than a producer of stress. A 1972 study of adult television watchers, conducted by the Society for Rational Psychology in Munich, showed that when some families give up TV, the effect is sometimes more aggression, an increased number of extramarital affairs and decreased interest in sex at home. The Society paid 184 habitual TV watchers not to watch; they were given a small sum for every day they did without the tube. None was able to hold out for longer than five months; nearly everyone reported heightened tension both inside and outside his family. While only 2 per cent of the husbands had ever beaten their wives before the experiment began and only 58 per cent of the parents had ever slapped their children, the incidence of such intra-family violence rose to 5 per cent and 66 per cent after the TV sets had darkened. The researchers did not claim, however, that TV eliminates family conflicts, only that it masks them, and that sometimes it can serve as a last link between generally estranged couples. "At least we have something in common we can talk about," some TV-watching husbands and wives told the experimenters.

Television has been a factor in ordinary life for only one generation, and its long-term effect on the family institution is difficult to forecast. But it seems almost certain to intensify the pressure on old-fashioned modes of living that began with the invention of printing and increased markedly with the world-wide spread of movies and radio. The stress imposed by the mass media almost inevitably leads to change. For the narrow and sometimes self-righteous way of traditional family life in all cultures depends to a large degree on ignorance of alternatives. As long as young people can be brought up thinking that their parents' mode is the only

The everyday frictions

When Bill Owens, a newspaper photographer who lives in a California town near San Francisco, set out to record the life style of his suburban neighbors, he found many scenes of family happiness and pleasure—and also some that reveal the stresses arising from the normal frictions of everyday affairs.

Five common stresses he pictured are reproduced here and on the following pages from his book, *Suburbia*, along with their original captions—the comments of his subjects. They were candid. The mother of the child at right, for example, says ruefully:

"I wanted Christina to learn some responsibility for cleaning her room, but it didn't work."

conceivable one, they can generally be counted on to repeat it. But isolation is next to impossible now. The whole world is receptive to the idea that there is another way of family life, open, less hidebound; that people can enjoy the here and now without always worrying about ancestral traditions and taboos. Having gotten the message, some societies have already altered both surface rituals and underlying beliefs. Eastern nations have accepted from Hollywood the courtship act of kissing (a filthy habit to old-fashioned Manuans, an unutterably lascivious one to Malaysians). Abominations like unchaperoned dating and unsupervised dancing, which once would have branded a girl as a whore, are accepted even by families in Spain and other conservative countries.

While television and other mass media bring outer world stresses into the home, the family generates many stresses of its own, without outside help. Under the best of circumstances individual members, possessing conflicting needs, desires and ambitions, are bound to grate against one another from time to time. The conflicts begin with the founders of the family, the marriage partners, who must make many adjustments to life together. They are intensified by personal disasters such as illness. And the pressures inevitably will be further exaggerated when the family must cope with in-laws or other relatives who are forced upon it by necessity rather than choice.

In-laws are such a common source of friction that the word defining the relationship is almost a synonym for familial strife. Yet the feeling about them is ambivalent. In-laws often are helpful in getting a marriage under way and in keeping it going. Frequently they arranged the meeting of the

"Every year I go to my mother-in-law's for Thanksgiving and every year I swear I'll never do it again. But I always do."

continued

couple in the first place. They provide marriage gifts, arrange for the church service, give helpful advice and sometimes even more helpful cash in time of difficulty. They are a refuge in times of storm. They can find John a job and Mary a baby sitter. But they also provide criticism and interference. The mother-in-law, in particular, can be a troublemaker of impressive dimensions.

All cultures recognize mothers-in-law as a potential source of strain in family life. It is estimated that almost two thirds of the world's societies set some kind of limits on contact with this specific relative. Westerners do not go to the lengths of the Ganda of Africa, who refuse to let a man speak to his mother-in-law. But the universality of the mother-in-law joke (as in the old one-liner: "Definition of conflict of interests: your mother-in-law drives over a cliff in your new Cadillac") is testimony to an awareness of mother-in-law trouble.

The success or failure of a marriage and its capacity for bearing stress depend mainly, however, not upon the presence or absence of in-laws or other sources of pressure, but upon the strength and flexibility of the relationship between the principal family figures: the husband and wife. In some cases the seeds of conflict are there from the start. The German poet Heinrich Heine once wrote, "The music at a wedding procession always reminds me of soldiers going into battle."

Although the hostilities are not necessarily overt, they are likely to be so on at least some occasions. Indeed, to some family experts, an absolutely smooth marital surface is too good to be true, a bad sign because it suggests hidden currents moving toward dangerous shoals. Strain is inev-

The everyday frictions *continued*

"I bought the Doughboy pool for David and the kids and now no one wants to take the responsibility for cleaning it."

itable, for no matter how close husband and wife may be in background, training, values and personality, there is certain to be some grinding of the gears when they try to mesh their lives together. In Hyman Rodman's lapidary phrase, "every marriage is a mixed marriage."

Some marriages, of course, are more mixed than others. In many parts of the world, both interfaith and interracial marriages have increased in recent years. A special U.S. Census Bureau study found that the number of American marriages matching a white partner with a non-white, though still relatively few, increased 63 per cent during the 1960s. Such marriages often work well, but they do pose special difficulties and require exceptional maturity from both spouses.

The same is true of interfaith marriages, where stress may be created less by broad doctrinal differences than by seemingly minor behavior patterns growing out of a particular religion. One social scientist cites the case of a Lutheran husband who had promised before marriage that he would neither interfere with his wife's Catholicism nor object to the raising of their children as Catholics. However, he had been born into a patriarchal German family in which a man's personal wishes were always catered to, and he was furious when his wife went to Mass at the very time he wanted her to serve him breakfast. He had never realized, he complained, that Catholicism is not only a faith but a whole way of living. To please him, his wife gave up morning church, but before long her deeply ingrained feeling that she ought to be attending Mass then was so strong that she began to feel extremely uneasy and therefore resentful toward the husband she saw as responsible for her discomfort.

Cooking dinner for six takes two hours. Then the kids inhale the food in minutes. After they are grown maybe they will remember the meals that their mother cooked."

continued

But while religion and race may be sources of stress for some couples, a more widespread source of discord is basic incompatibility between husband and wife, stemming from differences of temperament and personality that were obscured by romantic haze at the time of the marriage. For love is proverbially blind and the girl a man marries is not necessarily the one he saw the day he proposed. Besides, people often come to marriage with unrealistic expectations, imagining that the new partner will provide gratifications that parents once supplied—or failed to supply. As Yale psychiatrist Theodore Lidz puts it, "Every lover is something of a Pygmalion," fashioning, in fantasy, the perfect spouse. After the honeymoon comes the cold, continuing shower of reality. She is not quite the giving, motherly woman who will put up with his untidiness, wait on him hand and foot, and cook nothing but his favorite foods. He is not the carefree, adoring lover he appeared to be in courtship. When the reality of everyday life sets in, bringing an unbalanced checkbook and tears over thwarted wishes, both may begin to wonder what it was that they saw in each other. He may despair of understanding the one person whom he should know better than anybody else. The sardonic wit Ogden Nash posed the problem succinctly: "An occasionally lucky guess as to what makes a wife tick is the best a man can hope for. And even then, no sooner has he learned how to cope with the tick than she tocks."

The major disappointment in many marriages results from the roles the partners are required to play. Traditionally, society has defined very different roles for men and women—authoritarian for men, subordinate for women—and both sexes have accepted the type-casting that was thrust

The everyday frictions *continued*

"Basically we are very much alike, the same individual. Our temperaments however are different, we reflect on things differently. My son was raised to think for himself."

"My father is an ex-Army officer, I'm an ex-Marine. My life-style changes were hard for my dad to understand. I'm a freer individual, not different. He doesn't understand that."

upon them. But all this has been challenged in recent years. The women's liberation movement, with its effort to equalize sex status, has increased marital strain in cases in which husbands resent being asked to share household responsibilities and to help with traditionally feminine tasks. Family dissension may also result when wives seek fulfillment through careers rather than devote themselves exclusively to housekeeping. The potential for conflict is even greater when wives must remain at home even though they would prefer to work. A common case is the woman whose husband's business involves travel—while she stays home with the children and the cooking. His horizons widen while hers narrow. Inevitably, the changing perspectives reduce the area of compatibility between husband and wife. In some instances sexual conflicts may arise.

Sexual unhappiness of husbands and wives, many experts believe, is often simply a symptom of unresolved conflict in other areas. Sometimes one partner's sexual difficulty is a disguised expression of anger and revenge. As family sociologist Gerald Leslie says, a husband or wife who does not dare show open hostility can nevertheless hurt a spouse by failing, "unconsciously on purpose," to respond sexually.

One of the commonest outcomes of sexual incompatibility is adultery. Both the result of existing tension and a cause of still further conflict, adultery subjects the family to severe test because it threatens to split the family down the middle.

A few peoples, it is true, do not regard adultery as a serious breach in the family relationship, and accept sexual relations with other people's husbands or wives as a matter of course. Among the polar Eskimos, to cite one example, it was a matter of common politeness for a man to offer his guest the favors of his wife after dinner, and woe to the guest if he turned her down because she was toothless or smelled of walrus blubber; he might have gotten his brains knocked out for his squeamishness. The Lesu of New Guinea, too, often took a casual view of adultery—but not always. As Hortense Powdermaker wrote: "Some men are jealous, and some are not. Some men gladly accept the *tsera* (a gift) from their wives, who have received it from their lovers, and there is no rift in the family. Others, however, instead of taking the *tsera*, fight the wife's lover."

But most societies disapprove of adultery, especially for women. In fact, the double standard for sexual morality has been a subject of no little bitterness to women since the world began. In most cultures adultery is considered a far greater strain on the family fabric when it involves the wife than when it involves the husband. Julius Caesar could sleep with everyone from Cleopatra to the wife of Crassus, the richest Roman of the time, and no one minded, but one breath of rumor gave him grounds for putting aside his wife because, as he said, she had to be above suspicion. What is considered harmless philandering in the male may be the excuse for severe punishment in the female. Even if punishment is decreed for both, it is the woman who is apt to suffer more.

Various theoretical justifications have been offered for the double stan-

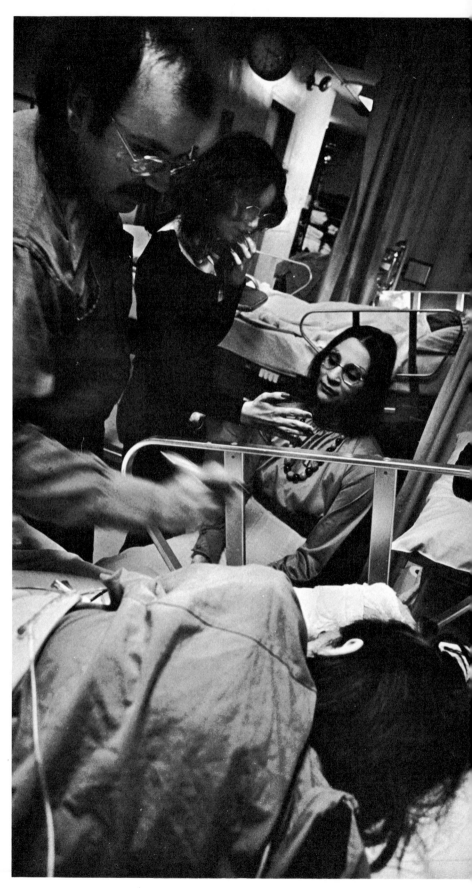

An anxious father, extending his hand toward the face of his barely conscious son, exhibits the emotional strain illness brings to a family. In the background the boy's sister tries to distract her mother from the wasting exhaustion of watching for a break in the child's condition.

dard, the most concise being the one sometimes attributed to the philosopher and psychologist William James (who reportedly said it came to him after an experiment with a psychedelic drug had brought a glimpse of the Secret of Existence):

Hogamous higamous
Man is polygamous,
Higamous hogamous
Woman's monogamous.

Recent changes in attitudes toward sex may have lessened the stigma attached to infidelity in marriage—and distributed more equitably whatever blame it brings. But whoever gets the blame and however far some cultures have moved toward sexual freedom, most people still take adultery seriously, in part because the feeling of sexual possessiveness that goes with marriage is deeply ingrained. In most families, adultery leads, at the very least, to bitter jealousies and intense bickering. More often than not, it also leads to painful self-reproaches, even among those who consider that they are liberated from traditional standards and reactions; many authorities doubt that spouses can accept their own or their partner's unfaithfulness with equanimity. In the words of psychoanalyst Robert Dorn, "Much as they may be taken with the idea of an affair, very few people can carry it off without grave feelings of remorse and guilt."

Beyond the sexual, financial and emotional stresses that families are exposed to lies the possibility that sudden disaster may strike, crippling the family and threatening its very survival. Probably the most catastrophic stress that a family can face is the serious illness of one of its members. If the sick person is the father, the family's livelihood may be at stake. A mother's illness may have even more serious consequences because, as Talcott Parsons expresses it, "she is the primary agent of supportive strength for the whole family."

If the mother is sick, the family may fall apart. Once more, it is the children who may be most seriously affected. Psychoanalyst Richard Gardner reports the case of a small boy whose reaction to learning that his mother had leukemia was a terrifying fantasy that he was drowning in quicksand. The same youngster was deeply disturbed by his belief, not unusual in a small child who cannot understand the physical causes of illness, that he, his sister and his father might be to blame for their mother's leukemia. Describing his own behavior, the little boy berated himself for "all the screaming I made," confessed that "me and my sister always give my mother trouble," and remembered a quarrel he had once witnessed during which "my Dad pushed my Mom against the refrigerator." Pitifully, he concluded that "I think it's all our fault."

If parental illness may shake a family to its foundations, so too can a child's grave illness. Every member of the family is profoundly affected —beginning, of course, with the sick child himself. More often than not, a child with a potentially fatal illness knows more about his prospects than adults imagine. When San Francisco psychiatrist Charles Binger and his

colleagues studied the families of 20 children who had died of leukemia in 1964 and 1965, they found that most of the sick children over four years of age, even those who were not told their diagnosis directly, "presented evidence to their parents that they were aware of the seriousness of their disease and even anticipated their premature death."

When parents have to spend a great deal of time with a hospitalized youngster, the result may be what psychiatrist Jesus Nahmias at Memorial Sloan-Kettering Cancer Center in New York City describes as fragmentation of family life. If the parents' marriage is at all shaky to begin with, the effect is most intense; if the marriage is strong, it can become even stronger. "Two people crying together can achieve real communication," Dr. Nahmias has found.

But for many the child's illness has the opposite effect. The father of a child who died of cancer when she was five has never forgotten the strain he and his wife felt during the child's long illness. "Your social life and your sex life are affected. You begin to feel, My God, on top of everything else, my marriage is going to the rocks." Many marriages do. The reasons are diverse. Psychiatrist Binger reports that fathers in his study "found many ways to absent themselves from painful involvement with their troubled families." Another divisive effect was noted by British clergyman Simon Stephens, founder of the Society of Compassionate Friends, which attempts to help the parents of dead or dying children. He asserts that fathers often try so hard "to keep a stiff upper lip because it's the British thing to do," that they show their wives little warmth and as a consequence, the stress may become intolerable.

When things get bad enough, a couple may begin looking for outside help not only in individual treatment but in family therapy. The patient is not one person alone but a whole family; sometimes three or even four generations come together in their therapist's office.

Increasing numbers of family therapists are beginning to equip their offices with cameras and are learning to operate them themselves so that they can record family talk sessions on videotape. The idea is to use the playback techniques familiar to TV sports fans so that each family member can get a good look at himself as he appears to the rest of the family. Very often husband or wife is shocked to observe in himself a facial expression, tone of voice or pattern of behavior of which he had been entirely unaware even though it was obvious—and distressing—to his partner. Watching a rerun of a discussion he has just had with his wife in their therapist's office, a husband may see that he habitually tries to blame his wife for their troubles, saying, "But you made me do it that way." Similarly, a wife may be forced by the evidence of the videotape to see that when her husband tries to discuss their conflicts, she changes the subject by answering, "I'll get back to that, but I want to point out that the other day . . ."

Psychiatrist Milton Berger of Manhattan, one of the pioneers in family therapy, describes one case in which a husband frequently listened to his wife with a judgmental look on his face, as if he were ready to pronounce her stupid. As the husband observed his own facial expression on tape, his wife told him that when he looked at her that way, "I don't know where I stand with you." The husband eventually came to realize that his own feelings of insecurity had led him to enjoy making his wife squirm under his critical look; subsequently he was able to change his behavior and reduce the strain in his marriage.

Berger finds that certain behavior patterns are common to many troubled marriages. For instance, the videotape recordings often show couples that things go wrong between them because they send contradictory "double messages" when they speak or listen. One husband responded to a suggestion from his wife by saying out loud, "That's a good idea." Yet at the same time, he brushed an invisible bit of dust from his trouser leg in such a way that his movement became a gesture of contemptuous dismissal. In another case a wife sat quietly listening to her husband speak, suggesting that she was paying close attention to him—yet her face looked bored and her gaze was directed over his shoulder.

Such insights into family conflicts may seem small, but can be decisive. They may enable a partner to change while there is still time. For the family it could mean the difference between surviving and cracking up.

The Bond Dissolved

A family is such a tough and resilient institution that it may crack and fissure in all directions and still hold together. The binding force may be complete devotion among family members. Or it may be a sense of duty, or sheer inertia, or a feeling that the rewards of companionship outweigh the handicaps. But then the day comes when nothing will hold a family together. Sometimes the provocation is traumatic: Mary finds a letter indicating that John has been unfaithful. Occasionally it is a final, insupportable irritation: Mary's cheerful little smile in the morning suddenly looks like an idiotic simper, or John's complaints about the bills finally become more than Mary can bear. From then on, total strangers look at each other across the breakfast table. The family has broken. Someone is going to leave.

For good or bad reasons, people are always leaving families. Teenagers run away, young people get married, old people move off to retirement homes. All these events may cause emotional anguish, but they do not destroy the basic structure of the family. That happens only when the nucleus itself splits, sundering the bond between the two principal family members, the father and the mother. Most such breaks are involuntary; they occur when death strikes husband or wife. The irrevocability of a tragedy of this sort can cause deep emotional disturbance among children, and leave the surviving spouse with a major adjustment to make. But many family ruptures come about voluntarily, when one spouse decides that he would prefer to go his separate way, or when both make a joint decision that they would do better to part. Such a break may seem less final than death, but it, too, can alter the texture of life, so both types of family dissolution have drawn scientists from many disciplines to study the customs surrounding them and the effects they have on individuals and societies.

The voluntary breakup of the family may take one of several forms—desertion, separation, annulment or divorce—but the situation each represents is both similar and universal. Almost every known society has recognized that circumstances may arise requiring an end to the family relationship. In ancient Rome, such prominent citizens as Cato, Sulla, Pompey, Caesar and Pliny the Younger were married and divorced as many as three to five times each. Even the Hebrew prophet Moses considered that divorce was sometimes permissible. The Law of Moses provided: "When a man hath taken a wife, and married her, and it comes to pass that she find no favor in his eyes, because he hath found some uncleanness in her: then let him write her a bill of divorcement, and give it in her hand, and send her out of his house."

Nowadays divorce is such a common phenomenon that many people consider it a runaway one. In the industrial countries, at least, divorce statistics have been rising more or less steadily for more than a century.

The reality may be less melodramatic than the statistics, however, and the frequency with which marriages break up may not have changed as much as the figures suggest. For one thing, it is much easier to get a legal divorce than it used to be. In Western countries until recently, divorce was either totally impossible (as in Italy) or extremely expensive and embarrassing, as in England and most of the United States. In addition, there was strong community disapproval of divorce and especially of the woman involved; divorcées were generally depicted in Victorian novels and in early Hollywood movies as little better than strumpets. Nevertheless, great numbers of people did get *de facto* divorces by slinking away in the dead of night, or by the simple process of walking out openly, slamming the door (like Nora in Ibsen's *A Doll's House*). These people were naturally not listed as divorced by the census taker, which is one reason why divorce figures for the 19th Century look abnormally low when they are compared with 20th Century ones. As a matter of fact, sociologist Talcott Parsons has estimated that the rate of marital breakup in the United States, including both desertion and divorce, has actually gone down in this century.

The widespread publicity given to the marital problems of American celebrities has led to the popular belief that the United States leads the world in divorces. It is true that an estimated one out of three marriages in the United States now ends in divorce. But the popular impression may involve some exaggeration, for no one compiles divorce statistics in many countries and the rate at which divorce is increasing in the United States is lower than in at least 15 other countries where such figures are collected. Sociologist William Goode notes that a majority of primitive societies have higher rates of marital dissolution than America does, and several nations in the past have at various times equaled or exceeded the present U.S. rate. Among the easygoing Alorese of Indonesia, for example, it is estimated that half the men and more than a third of the women have been divorced at least once. Certain Eskimo women think nothing of getting married and divorced several times a year.

Such statistics and broad studies indicate the general stability or instability of the family in an entire culture, and they cannot predict how any particular marriage is going to turn out. But certain figures do provide some interesting insights into the kinds of marriage that are more likely to turn sour.

Some of these insights serve to confirm widespread impressions. For example, teen-age marriages are more likely to break up than those contracted later in life, bearing out the popular belief that teenagers are too immature to establish permanent family relationships. But the statistics also showed a marked increase in divorce among the middle-age group. The reason may be increased longevity. Better health care means that people between 45 and 60 are still vigorous enough to begin a new life if they decide that they want to.

*sin long associated with divorce is
veyed in this turn-of-the-century
ter—a father, who has been awarded
tody of his child by a satanic
ge, drags the heartbroken little girl
y from her distraught mother.*

There are, however, a number of genuine surprises among the statistics. Surprise number one is that the probability of divorce is doubled when couples have children during the first year of marriage. This finding goes directly contrary to folk wisdom, which holds that newlyweds should have a baby as soon as possible to bind their relationship. But the fact is that newly married couples often are too unsettled to face the added strain of child rearing before they have had time to work out their own problems; the arrival of a baby may drive them apart instead of bringing them together as they had hoped.

The second surprise relates to the economic backgrounds of the people who are being divorced. Popular opinion, distorted no doubt by publicity from the world's divorce capitals, holds that divorce is an amusement of the idle rich. But popular opinion is wrong once again, for the figures actually show that marriages are more likely to come apart among poor people than among those who are rich. Living together is hard enough at best, and it is all the harder when it must be done in cramped quarters with no assurance of where next month's rent is coming from or how the grocery bill is to be paid. In addition, some poor people are brought up with less respect for the sanctity of marriage; there is less pressure on them not to disgrace the family by divorce and they find it correspondingly simpler to break their marriage vows.

If poverty does not necessarily hold a marriage together, neither does a love match. There is more likelihood of divorce when there is free marital choice than when marriages are arranged by the parents. This cultural difference might seem to be a tribute to the superior wisdom of older people, but experts are inclined to believe that it reflects the lower expectations of partners in an arranged marriage. Romantics who think they are entering on a life of permanent bliss, or at least of loving companionship, are most apt to be disillusioned by a loveless marriage and to resort to divorce so they can look elsewhere for a fulfilling relationship.

Perhaps the biggest surprise of all has to do with the effect of marital conflicts. Most people assume that there is a close link between conflicts and divorce. But a study by John Cuber and Peggy Haroff suggests that quarrelsome spouses are no more likely to break up than congenial ones. The two researchers classified couples in categories that ranged from the most argumentative to a group they called "total," meaning closely united. In the conflict-habituated marriages, "incompatibility is pervasive, conflict is ever potential, an atmosphere of tension permeates the togetherness." The totals, on the other hand, worked and played together; "all as-

*In Rome's Piazza Navona in 1970,
demonstrators bearing huge placards of
the Italian Divorce League (L.I.D.)
protest Italy's strict divorce law.
Opponents of the divorce ban agitated for
92 years before they finally gained
a limited relaxation of the law in 1974.*

pects of life were mutually shared and enthusiastically participated in."
It would be reasonable to expect a high divorce rate in the first group, a
low one in the second. But Cuber and Haroff found that the totals were just
as apt to split up as the others, presumably on account of the intensity of
their relationship. It is possible to imagine a husband coming home, say,
with lipstick on his shirt collar. For Mrs. Conflict-habituated, this might
be only one more pretext for one of the shrill declamatory and crockery-
throwing sessions on which the couple depends for emotional sustenance.
For Mrs. Total, on the other hand, any leak in the dike of affection could
mean the floodwaters are coming in and it's all over.

Pressures within the family itself, however, seem to influence the likelihood of divorce less than those outside. One of the most significant factors
is the attitude society takes, the degree of importance it gives to marital stability. Here, too, there are surprises. Statistics in Western countries have
shown a rise in the divorce rate parallel to the mass movement of country
people to the cities. At first, scholars assumed that divorce was a direct result of industrialization, that stable farm families break up when exposed
to the fragmented world of factories and big cities. Then the experts observed exceptions in non-Western countries, notably in 19th Century Japan
and 20th Century Algeria, where the divorce rates fell drastically after a
predominantly rural population began to move to the cities. In both nations, it soon became clear, the explanation was the same. Among
traditional country people, attitudes toward the marriage bond were fairly lackadaisical; when people grew tired of each other, they got a divorce,
with no bad blood on either side. But when they moved to urban areas,
they began to model their behavior on that of the upper classes, which had
much more rigorous notions about marital stability, considering it both a
religious and social necessity for families to stay together. So the sons and
daughters of peasants began to consider that marriage was a sacred contract that ought not to be broken lightly, and the divorce rate among them
soon went down.

Some cultures are even more relaxed in their attitudes toward divorce
than oldtime Japanese and Algerian farmers. They show no concern as to
whether husbands and wives stay together or not. Among a great variety
of peoples in widely separated parts of the world—the Aymara of Bolivia
and Peru, the Reindeer Chukchee of Siberia, the Ojibways of Canada, the
Pukapukas of Polynesia—there are no barriers, legal or otherwise, to divorce; if a marriage fails to work, man and wife can go their separate
ways by simply saying goodbye.

But these attitudes are exceptional. Most societies require certain formalities before a divorce is recognized, even if the ritual is no more
complicated than the "I divorce thee," thrice repeated, which does the
trick in some Islamic countries. In many societies there are economic and
social restraints on people who might otherwise opt for divorce. The bride
price may have to be paid back to the husband's parents if she leaves
home, an unpleasant prospect for the wife's family. H. Ian Hogbin reports

of the Melanesian Wogeo that a wife will rarely initiate divorce proceedings because under Wogeo law her husband will keep the children. Dorothea Leighton and Clyde Kluckhohn describe how Navaho families customarily put great pressure on warring spouses to stay together. This is because they "see in a marriage that fails a threat not only to original investment, but to future good feeling and cooperation of all types between the two families. . . . The elders and all the brothers and sisters involved do their best to reconcile the estranged pair, and each side admonishes its representative to mend his or her ways."

In Western society the past few generations have seen a change amounting to a revolution in the attitude toward divorce. It would have been unthinkable for a divorced man to be a serious candidate for the U.S. Presidency before, say, World War II. But by the time Adlai Stevenson was running in 1952, the issue was hardly raised, and it is doubtful if a majority of voters even knew he had been divorced.

This more relaxed view has become characteristic of religious as well as of secular groups. During the 1920s, the Methodist Church did not permit its ministers to marry a divorced person unless he had been the innocent spouse in a marriage broken by adultery. Forty years later, the same church required only that the divorcé understand why his first marriage had failed and that he resolve to do better on his second try. And while the Roman Catholic Church as a whole has made no essential change in its stance on divorce, notable individuals within its hierarchy have done so. In 1973, Monsignor Stephen J. Kelleher, past presiding Judge of the Marriage Tribunal of the Archdiocese of New York, published a book called *Divorce and Remarriage for Catholics?* It maintains that troubled unions can prevent human growth, and it suggests that not everyone should be expected to live up to doctrinal pronouncements about the indissolubility of the marriage bond.

These changing attitudes are paralleled by changing laws. In most places, grounds for divorce were very restrictive until recently. As a matter of fact, in many American states the only ground was adultery. The adultery had to be proved (generally by connivance) and one party had to be branded the guilty one. The current trend is toward what is called no-fault divorce, in which neither partner is stigmatized for failure, no specific offense is charged, and a union is ended simply because of "incompatibility," "irreconcilable differences" or "insupportability." By 1974, all but eight states had passed laws permitting divorces in which neither partner was blamed for the breakup. As a result, many people who might have drawn back from the often squalid squabbles connected with the older types of divorce action became willing to take the new and simpler legal steps leading to freedom.

A similar change has taken place in England, where a reform law that went into effect in 1971 greatly liberalized the divorce requirements. Previously, adultery and cruelty had been the only practical grounds for divorce. The new law added desertion and separation, and brought a sharp increase in the number of British divorces—from 28,376 in 1962 to 118,253 a decade later.

Divorce Italian style came very slowly. The country's strict prohibition against divorce finally was eased in 1972 after a bitter struggle that lasted almost a century. But even now the grounds are limited to incurable insanity, nonconsummation of the marriage, desertion, or proof that the marriage partner is either sexually perverted or a criminal who has been sentenced to life in prison.

In many places the more relaxed attitude toward the increasing social acceptability of divorce and the simplification of procedures are bound up with a third important factor: the improved status of women. Because most 19th Century women lived on farms, had little or no education and had almost never held a job of any kind, divorce might well have left them stranded, with children to bring up and no possible way of supporting them. Today, wives have become less dependent on their husbands. As Goode points out, a divorced woman can now support herself, even though her salary may be considerably smaller than her husband's was.

All of these considerations make the recent rise in the divorce rate seem somewhat less ominous than the prophets of doom would have it. Far from portending the demise of the family, some experts maintain, a high divorce rate is actually a sign of faith in the family and in its possibilities. People get divorced not because they are disillusioned about marriage but precisely because they have come to expect so much from it. A high divorce rate, says anthropologist Paul Bohannan, "means that the quality of the family is improving. If we don't measure up to the higher standards that we're imposing on ourselves, at least we try again rather than compromising as our grandparents did. As long as quality rises, you're going to have a larger percentage of failures."

One manifestation of such faith in the family is the frequency with which divorced people remarry—disregarding Samuel Johnson's somewhat cynical dictum that a second marriage represents the triumph of hope over experience. A large majority of ex-spouses—more than two thirds, according to Goode's research—take new spouses within a fairly short time. Many of these remarriages were in fact planned in advance, and may have been one of the main reasons for getting the divorce in the first place. Even for those who have made no such plans, both social and psychological pressures to remarry are very strong. Only the remarkably small proportion of 3.4 per cent described themselves as presently divorced in the 1973 figures from the U.S. Bureau of the Census. What happened to all the others who had been through the divorce courts? Presumably they had moved on to new marriages.

However common divorce may be, and however little it may alter the overall pattern of family living, it remains a serious matter in the lives of the individuals involved. It can be a traumatic experience, as people who have been through it attest and as studies by many sociologists confirm. Divorce hurts, and the fact that many other people are in the same boat helps not at all. Says Harvard sociologist Robert Weiss, "Divorce is more like influenza than like unemployment. If everybody is unemployed, it makes it a little easier. If everyone has the flu, you still feel just as sick." It should be added, however, that like the flu, divorce is rarely fatal. Most people seem to recover, sometimes with amazing resiliency; in some fortunate circumstances they even grow psychologically as a result of their experience.

During the months of sickness that precede recovery, the wife is traditionally the center of the emotional disturbance caused by divorce. She may be quite crushed; she may feel hopelessly adrift without the person whom, in most cases, she has come to regard as her psychological support and her economic provider. If her husband initiated the parting, she will feel angry; if she asked for divorce, she may suffer from feelings of guilt. Or she may have the ambivalent reaction described by Weiss as fairly typical of divorcées, swinging between euphoria and depression. Many women, he says, greet freedom with elation; they "go around several feet off the ground. They feel they can do anything, that nothing can touch them." Then elation gives way to despair, to feelings of regret and inadequacy. They have to fit themselves into a new category, that of the divorced woman, and as Goode puts it, there is no clear-cut, accepted model for such a woman in our society. A bride knows where she stands: she is expected to go and live with her husband and share his life. But what does a divorced woman do? Does she go home to mother, does she keep her old friends, does she move to a new town? What name does she use, what does she do with her time?

The divorcée's role is particularly difficult because she must remake her social life at the same time that she is trying to cope with the petty problems of daily life. Women friends who rallied round solicitously at first may soon cut her off because they consider her a potential rival. When she begins seeing other men, she may resent having to return to adolescent patterns of dating, and she may find it hard to be a mother and an eligible woman at the same time. What is she to tell her children about the men she goes out with?

For many divorcées, however, the picture is not that bleak. When Goode questioned 425 divorced women in Detroit, he found that 37 per cent had not suffered seriously after divorce. Only 30 per cent felt they had been discriminated against as divorcées, more than half reported that they had been able to keep their old friends, and most of the others said they had succeeded in making new friends.

Ex-husbands as well as ex-wives are hurt by divorce. They too have problems of guilt over failure, of feeling bereaved even though they would not wish to resume the marriage, of experiencing a drop in self-esteem. The men are often unhappy about their usually diminished role in their children's lives, although some youngsters, of course, continue to live with their fathers after the divorce.

In America in recent years, more and more fathers have been asking

This German worker, disconsolately sitting with his little boy at their kitchen table, is one of the increasing number of men the world over who have been deserted by their wives. His wife walked out on him one day without even leaving a letter behind. During the day a neighbor cares for his son, but in the evenings and on weekends he must stay at home to look after the child and try to make up for the absence of his wife.

for and winning custody of their children. This has not always been true elsewhere. In China in the past, divorced men usually kept their children, but since the implementation of the marriage law of 1950, more and more wives are being given custody.

The changing pattern in the United States causes special adjustment problems, particularly for fathers who suddenly find themselves bearing the burden of caring for their children. Lou Filczer, president of a counselling service for men in Chicago, who was awarded custody of his 14-year-old son, explains: "I had to learn a little about that other role, being around and being more responsive to his presence," Filczer admitted. "It was tough, but we made it." His success is still rare; generally children are left in their mother's care. Although the fathers may see their offspring frequently, they must nevertheless resign themselves to the fact that their ex-wives are almost certain to exert the decisive influence on the children's developing personalities.

Psychological and emotional dislocations are only part of the problem facing divorced men. Their financial situation, too, can become desperate if they are saddled with heavy alimony payments. Alimony, a monetary

payment to a former wife to make up for the loss of her husband, is an accepted feature of life in Europe and America, but it is almost unknown elsewhere in the world. William N. Stephens, in *The Family in Cross-Cultural Perspective*, could find only two other societies that provide for it: the Copper Eskimo and the Iban of Borneo.

The one-sidedness of alimony has been moderated in recent years by the women's liberation movement. The states of California and New York now permit ex-husbands to sue their divorced wives for financial maintenance. California even discards the word alimony; its law speaks instead of "spousal support." Despite these innovations, it is still mostly men who pay alimony, often a disproportionate share of their income. Some divorced women demand huge payments, not so much out of greed, Willard Waller has suggested, but in an attempt to make it economically impossible for their former husbands to remarry. And since alimony ceases on the recipient's remarriage, a divorcée has a financial incentive to remain single, prolonging both the payments and her husband's inability to afford a new marriage.

If divorce creates complex problems for both husbands and wives, they can at least feel that, as adults, they had alternatives, that they deliberately chose to face these problems. Not so for the children involved in divorce. They have no say in the matter. It is popularly believed that they are the ones who suffer most from the splitting up of a marriage, and that they may be overwhelmed by the consequences of divorce. Uncounted marriages are held together solely by fear that breakup would cause irreparable harm to the offspring.

Little research has been done on this subject, and findings are so far inconclusive. But whether or not divorce causes permanent harm to children, it undoubtedly causes them pain. They are rarely in a position to understand its causes or ramifications, and for that reason they may be obsessed with an irrational fear that they were at fault. It is easy for them to conclude that the parent who is leaving home does not love them, and they may be left with another irrational fear, that they will never be loved again. Children are often used as pawns by their parents, each battling for the youngsters' affection. They may be encouraged to stage scenes, to make life difficult, to spy—to keep one parent posted about how much money the other parent spends and whom he sees. Frequently a lonely mother makes outrageous emotional demands on a small child, expecting a son to make up, in effect, for the loss of her husband. Even in the most amicable of divorces, the children are left with a sudden gap in their existence, an abrupt change in the most intimate part of their lives.

Just how unsettling the absence of a parent can be was indicated in a well-known study by criminologists Sheldon and Eleanor Glueck, *Unraveling Juvenile Delinquency*. The Gluecks reported that children are much more likely to be delinquent if they come from broken homes than if they come from intact ones. But the word broken covers a multitude of categories. Somewhat to their surprise, the Gluecks found that children who had lost one parent through death were more apt to be delinquent than those who had lost one through divorce. And the rates were still higher for children from "separated" homes, that is, families in which the parents were living apart but still interacting unhappily with each other and avoiding the clean break of a divorce.

A Swedish study by Gustav Jonsson parallels the Gluecks' research in America. Comparing delinquent with nondelinquent boys, it showed that 41 per cent of the delinquent boys came from broken homes as opposed to only 13 per cent of the nondelinquent ones. But when Jonsson went on to analyze his cases in a different way he noticed a curious phenomenon. He looked closely at the nondelinquent boys, those who came from broken homes together with those who were from intact homes. And he found it was impossible, at least by any of the tests that he used, to tell which of the nondelinquent boys had divorced parents and which ones had not. Their attitudes and behavior patterns appeared to be identical. One of his conclusions was that the vital factor was not divorce itself but the way the parents adjusted afterward. The parents of the nondelinquent boys were found to have made the transition successfully, even if not always smoothly. In the families of the delinquent boys, on the other hand, the stress and strain of the predivorce period had carried over: the mother had perhaps never married again and was still embittered about her experience as a wife; or she had married a man who did not get on well with her children; or the boy was shifted back and forth between antagonistic parents.

Jonsson's findings suggest some of the perils of easy generalizations about children's attitudes and reactions to divorce. After some 295 university students whose parents had been divorced years before were interviewed by the sociologist Judson Landis, he reported that close to 40 per cent had no memory at all of having suffered because of the divorce. Of the others, about one fifth remembered that as children they had experienced feelings of shame because of the fact that their parents were divorced, while one out of six had felt inferior to other children. Almost half felt that they had been used by one or both parents after the divorce, often by attempts to play on their sympathy or to get them involved in continuing quarrels. Among those who came from openly unhappy homes, more than half considered that divorce had been the best thing for everyone concerned. Those from homes where the parents had pretended up to the last moment that everything was rosy, that they were all one happy family, were the ones who suffered most from the rude shock of awakening to reality and from the changes that followed the divorce of their parents. Landis also discovered that the students who were experiencing adolescent difficulties in adjustment came less often from families broken by divorce than from homes where the parents had either separated or stayed together in an atmosphere of continual conflict.

From this and from other studies, as well as from the observations of psychiatrists, social workers and other experts who work with children, it would seem that a break between parents may, initially at least, be a shat-

Society often lends a helping hand to the family that is shattered by divorce or death. The Japanese mother and her child at left live in one of the cluttered but comfortable apartments provided for fatherless families such as theirs by the Tokyo Metropolitan Government. In the United States, numerous groups help divorced and widowed people rebuild their lives. Below, members of a Brooklyn, New York, branch of Parents Without Partners help celebrate a child's birthday.

tering blow to children. But the fact is that the family is a highly resilient institution, able to survive even the rudest shocks, pull its fragments together, and go on living and performing its normal functions. It seems quite clear, for example, that the effects of divorce are likely to be less severe than those of prolonged strife and mutual irritation between parents who insist on trying to keep the home intact. Children are apt to be tougher and more realistic than sentimental parents sometimes give them credit for. They often face up to divorce situations with what may seem to their parents surprising maturity; conversely, when parents show some maturity in coping with divorce and its aftermath, some experts believe that children learn from example how best to meet difficult situations.

The same resiliency that marks the family in divorce is to be found when it confronts a much more drastic cleavage: death. Death, of course, contradicts the principle of continuity that is the essence of the family; and every family in every culture has to work out methods of meeting its supreme challenge.

The heaviest blow may fall on the children, as is suggested by the Gluecks' finding that the death of a parent is more likely to create emotional disturbance in children than a divorce. It is easy to see why. Divorced parents, even if they involve the children in custodial battles or emotional tugs-of-war, are still there to love their children and to protect them. The children continue to have a father and a mother they can relate to. But death leaves a frightening sense of loss; something the youngsters thought eternal has dropped irrevocably out of their lives.

The strain on the surviving spouse, of course, is also very great. For the death of a husband or wife tears up the family fabric. Both behavioral studies and simple statistics testify to the difficulty of readjustment. Widows and widowers have a higher mortality rate than do married people and they run a greater risk of developing emotional troubles. Grief may exhaust them physically, leaving them prey to serious illness. Their depression very often worsens ailments they already have; sufferers from diabetes and hypertension are particularly affected. Bereaved husbands and wives have a high suicide rate, too. And even if they do not kill themselves outright, New York psychiatrist Alvin Goldfarb has noted, they sometimes engage in behavior that is basically suicidal: eating and drinking far too much, driving their cars too fast, even provoking attack by actively resisting muggers on city streets.

To recover from grief, say the experts, the surviving spouse must detach his emotions from the person who is gone, renounce the husband or wife role he had filled, and master an entirely different role, that of the widow or widower. Those who make the transition successfully usually go through three stages: denial, depression and recovery. In the first, they try to wipe out the reality of death by denying, unconsciously, that it has really occurred. In his 1972 book *Bereavement: Studies of Grief in Adult Life,* British psychiatrist Colin Parkes explained that denial can be seen in the tendency of widows and widowers to imagine they have just seen their

dead spouses. One British widow confided, "I think I catch sight of him in his van, but it's the van from down the road." When a sociologist studied widows in Dorchester, Massachusetts, another kind of denial was found. Several women revealed that it had taken them a year to change their food-shopping habits—to buy for a family of three, for instance, instead of a family of four.

Under the impact of reality, the process of denial eventually stops working and the surviving husband or wife has no choice but to understand that his loss is final. That is the period when depression sets in, in many instances compounded by guilt or anger. Parkes recounts one case in which a widow felt overwhelming guilt for a trivial failure: she had never made her husband a bread pudding. He also tells of a woman who raged at her dead husband, saying that if he had known what it was like, he would never have left her.

After a period of months, the stage of recovery begins, and with it the effort to establish a new life. But even when widows and widowers are emotionally ready to do so, they may not find it so easy to make new friends or stay close to old ones. Parkes learned that every bereaved wife encounters people who become uneasy in her presence, "as if the widow has become tainted with death." In some primitive cultures, the stigma of widowhood is openly acknowledged; certain peoples regard widows as contaminated beings and condemn them to the lonely existence of pariahs. The Shuswap of British Columbia, says A. L. Cochrane in a paper called "A Little Widow is a Dangerous Thing," isolate their widows and widowers and forbid them to touch their own bodies. The Agutainos of Polawan hold that the mere sight of a widow will induce death. To prevent this, Cochrane explains, a widow "may only go out at an hour when she is unlikely to meet anyone." Even then, she "knocks with a wooden peg on the trees as she goes along, warning people of her presence. It is believed that the very trees on which she knocks will soon die."

Less superstitious cultures—the ancient Jews, and many preliterate peoples of today—make it simple for a widow to begin a new existence; they provide that she marry her husband's brother (a custom known as the levirate) or that the widower marry his wife's sister (the sororate).

Even where there are no such formal rules, the outer and inner pressures to find a new mate are generally very strong, at least as strong as in the case of divorced persons. The widower often needs a wife to bring up children of his first marriage, and perhaps to bear him others. The widow may feel that she needs a man to protect and provide for her and for her children. In any case, both need companionship, and both want a sexual partner. For as modern research shows, sexual urges do not ordinarily slacken off to zero, whatever the age of the surviving husband or wife. Of widows, sex researcher William Masters observes, "they have this incredible need to be with men, and they do something about it. In many instances the man is married. Women who wouldn't consider cheating on a marriage, once that marriage is terminated, don't feel so strongly about that anymore." Paul Gebhard of the Indiana Institute for Sex Research reports that most widows who manage to find new sexual partners do so in the first year of widowhood, and he adds, "there is no lack of men willing to solace a new widow."

When it comes to remarrying, however, the widow's chances are considerably smaller than those of the widower. One simple reason is the longevity of women in most societies. According to 1971 figures, the life expectancy for women in the United States is seven and a half years greater than that for men. One result, of course, is an overabundance of widows. There are four times as many widows as widowers, giving a considerable advantage to the men who, besides, do not have to worry about public ridicule if they marry women much younger than themselves. About 45 per cent of widowers are believed to remarry. For widows, a study by Gebhard shows, the figure is only about 27 per cent. What keeps the percentage down for both sexes is not merely lack of opportunity but a phenomenon that Gebhard describes as chains to the cemetery. The term means emotional ties to the dead. Because of them, Gebhard explains, many a bereaved spouse finds that no one can possibly measure up to his or her image of a former wife or husband—partly because that image "tends to benefit from selective memory."

The thousands of men and women who do not succeed in finding new partners must fend for themselves for the rest of their lives. The lucky ones among them establish active and productive lives by establishing new relationships. Betty Wilson, a Boston widow whose husband died in 1961 after a three-year battle with cancer, is one of those who did. "In my kind of marriage," she said, "you had a permanent and total commitment to one person. I now have temporary and partial commitments to many people. It is not what you had, but it can be a very fulfilling life." For less resilient women, widowhood may be a lonely preparation for the grave.

Such gloomy prospects are only one aspect of a subtle change in the way people view death. In times past it was accepted as inevitable. Today it is pushed out of mind; everyone does his best to avoid the subject. A French sociologist has suggested that every society needs to characterize something as obscene, not proper to be mentioned unless veiled in circumlocutions. For Victorian grandparents it was sex; for the present generation it is death.

Still, even the most modern family cannot hope to avoid death. People may arrange to die in discreetly isolated nursing homes, drugged enough to make no indecent noise that would disturb visiting children. Their relatives may deposit their bodies beneath unostentatious gravestones in cemeteries that are designed to look like meadows or like beautiful parks. But everyone does die nevertheless. And drawn by some feeling of guilt or duty, of affection or reverence, or by the wish to listen to the reading of the will, or by a simple, atavistic sense of family continuity, kinsmen will generally show up to see their relatives off. In fact, funeral attendance is perhaps a final tribute to the strength of family ties. It may be only a slight exaggeration to say that in many cases almost the only genuine family reunions these days take place in graveyards: distant cousins with whom the dead person quarreled, and broke, ages ago, and in-laws who never bothered to turn up for Christmas dinner or a wedding celebration will come from miles away to see a member of the family return to Mother Earth.

Imperfect Alternatives

7

Ever since men first began to analyze their affairs in a systematic way, philosophers and theorists of various stripes have been seeking a viable alternative to the family. Puzzled and annoyed by the illogical muddle of family life, they have pointed to clean and sensible ways in which, theoretically, life could be organized. As early as the Fifth Century before Christ, the Greek thinker Plato was finding fault with the family and proposing that parents relinquish their babies as soon as they were born and allow the state to bring them up.

When Plato was given a chance to put his theories into actual practice, in Syracuse, he got nowhere at all. Of course, he lived in a world that was, by comparison with contemporary standards, hopelessly backward in both technology and administrative techniques: surely, it would seem, modern man can do better.

But in fact, no one has yet found a lasting, workable alternative to the family, and there is little prospect that success in the future will replace the failure of the past. Nevertheless, the family will inevitably continue to change. Child-caring functions are being modified as outside agencies provide more services to help families rear their young. And affectional functions, which are now lacking in some families and are peripheral rather than central in others, are being accentuated, as love and a sense of belonging become ever more crucial in an increasingly impersonal society. These two trends were first discernible some generations ago, and they are likely to continue into the future.

If the family fills such essential purposes so well, and adapts so readily to changing circumstances, it seems strange that anyone would try to do away with it. Plato marshaled two main arguments against the family, and he stated both with admirable power and brevity in *The Republic*. The first can be called the argument from efficiency. The family, Plato believed, is an absurdly wasteful, clumsy device for raising children. When people want to produce good hounds, he noted, they choose the sires and dams and then train the pups through a rational series of exercises to perform the tasks of adult life. By contrast, in Plato's view, children are bred indiscriminately and brought up helter-skelter, without a systematic plan for inculcating the virtues required of citizens in a well-run state. Plato's second argument against the family was that it is immoral because it is so

profoundly selfish and self-centered. He explained that when people live in a family, they think first of the family's good, and only second, or not at all, of the well-being of the state as a whole.

These arguments have been taken up and elaborated over the past 2,400 years. As recently as 1958, Harvard professor Barrington Moore, Jr. asked indignantly: "Are we to regard as permanent and natural a civilization that develops its most advanced techniques for killing people and leaves their replacement to the methods of the Stone Age?"

Plato's argument from morality has also been pressed home by others. Monogamy, said John Humphrey Noyes in the 1840s, "makes a man or woman unfit to practice the two central principles of Christianity, loving God and loving one's neighbor." One currently fashionable school of thought, associated with the British psychoanalyst R. D. Laing, accuses the family of deliberately murdering all that is creative and spontaneous in the individual. In a book appropriately called *The Death of the Family*, a disciple of Laing's named David Cooper says that the family glues together stunted, incomplete people who pass their inadequacies on to their children. Besides, Cooper charges, the family imposes roles on people in a rigid, unimaginative way, and forces children into "surface rituals like etiquette, organized games, mechanical learning operations," instead of leaving them to "spontaneous creativity, inventive play, freely developing fantasies and dreams."

Overstated though these arguments quite obviously are, they do contain some nuggets of truth, or at least of plausibility. The steady progress of modern society toward a more rational organization of its life and its efforts has already deprived the typical family of many of its traditional functions—economic, religious, educational and so on. It can reasonably be contended that further technological progress should make it possible to relieve the family of its last remaining vital functions, the physical care and the socialization of its children.

It can also be contended that great numbers of people already live outside a family context. Soldiers and sailors, monks and nuns, whores and gigolos, homosexuals, lunatics, tramps, loners of all sorts, live-in maids, orphans in asylums, convicts in prisons, alcoholics on skid row—all in their different ways, some approved by society and some condemned, lead nonfamilial lives.

These facts have led innumerable reformers since Plato's day to try to abolish the family or at least to diminish its role. Some have insisted that a single parent was sufficient for child rearing, but in most cases the goal was to replace the family with a commune, a larger group in which the love and loyalty of individual members would be directed toward the group as a whole rather than toward their own parents or children or relations. So far, such efforts have had a notable lack of success. The reasons for their failure are fairly obvious. A change in the traditional family system can come about in only two ways: a nationwide change enforced by the superior authority of the state, or a voluntary grouping of individuals within

149

a larger community that remains familial. There are major roadblocks on both routes to a communal way of life.

Despite fearsome powers of coercion and efficient propaganda, no modern state has succeeded in legislating the family out of existence. The Bolshevik revolutionaries who seized power in Russia in 1917 were doctrinaire Marxists who believed that marriage was a form of prostitution and that the family must die under Socialism. In the first flush of their experimental passion, they tried to undermine the foundations of family life. They decreed that marriage was unnecessary, recognized no difference between legitimate and illegitimate children and made both abortion and divorce simple to obtain. They sought to deprive the family of its role in socializing children, attacked the authority of parents and even tried to induce youngsters to spy on mothers and fathers whose revolutionary zeal fell short of Soviet standards.

All of the government's efforts, especially the attempt to bring up children apart from their parents, came to grief. The divorce rate rose so high, and the birth rate fell so low, that even blasé Soviet officials were alarmed. Parents were grief-stricken at enforced separation from their children. As one factory worker acknowledged to a social scientist, "We have a great need for boarding nurseries, but the fact that my son is becoming alienated from me is so painful that I can't even talk about it. I call him, 'Sasha, my son.' But he just runs away. No! I have to spend at least an hour or two each day with my son. Otherwise, it's impossible; otherwise, I can't stand it."

Russian social scientists themselves have agreed that families are uniquely qualified to rear children because the love of parents for their offspring creates the best possible atmosphere for learning. One study of Soviet youngsters raised in institutions instead of at home concluded that children brought up outside their families often became one-sided or retarded. Another result was a marked rise in what the Soviets called "hooliganism," or juvenile delinquency. Between 1929 and 1935, there was so much vandalism, theft, rape and murder by youthful offenders that the juvenile delinquency rate nearly doubled.

As a result, the Soviet government did an about-face, completely abandoning its attempt to do away with the family. For all the twistings of the party line, the trend since the 1930s has been in the direction of conservatism. Homosexuality has been outlawed, abortion discouraged, divorce made difficult, illegitimate children branded, faithfulness and togetherness emphasized in official propaganda. Though Russian family life has been profoundly modified under the Communist regime, chiefly by taking women out of the home and sending them into the factories, the institution still exists; and sociologist Gerald Leslie finds in fact that the Russian family has become much like the American family.

The Chinese Communists, too, have shaken the family system of their country but have not destroyed it. They have not tampered very much with the relationship between parents and children. What they have tried to do

Goodbyes after a beach party begin with an embrace as the man above prepares to leave other members of his "artificially extended family." A group composed of unrelated adults with their children, it is part of an experimental extension of the nuclear family undertaken by the Unitarian Church of Santa Barbara, California. The members provide one another the mutual support of the old-fashioned multigeneration family, sharing decision making, baby-sitting and chores as well as social activities.

is to substitute the commune for the *tsu,* that is, the old clan or extended family with its Confucian ideals of tight loyalties among kinsmen, reverence for the patriarch and total subservience of women. Although there are pockets of resistance, the government has generally had considerable success in this limited objective. When a Western journalist paid a visit in 1973 to Chen Chi-fun and his family, prosperous peasants who belong to the Kwang Li People's Commune in Kwangtung Province, she found a portrait of party Chairman Mao in the spot where a traditional Chinese family would have installed pictures of their ancestors as well as an altar to worship them. Everywhere, the same journalist found the effects of the 1950 Marriage Law. Under this statute arranged marriages are banned, mothers-in-law are forbidden to tyrannize young wives, women are permitted to divorce their husbands and legally sanctioned male dominance over women is brought to an end.

Under the Chinese Communist regime, children officially belong to the state, which assumes the responsibility of educating them in Communist doctrine from infancy on. Nevertheless, as in the Soviet Union, the Chinese government expects parents to carry out some of this indoctrination in the home. As a matter of fact, Cornell psychologist Urie Bronfenbrenner believes that the Chinese family still performs the chief function of families everywhere, the socialization of children. And sociologist William Goode reports that despite the recent proliferation of nurseries, old-age homes and the like, Chinese families are still considered duty bound to look after their members. As one Communist party document said not long ago, "Arrangements made by a housewife in feeding the old and teaching the young, making every member of her family feel comfortable, will naturally lighten the burden on the society and the collective." Indeed the liberated wife of Chen Chi-fun, like a good many of her female compatriots on the Kwang Li People's Commune, still prepares most of her family's meals. At lunchtime, everyone comes home from work or school and gathers at a round dining table in the living room of the family's red brick home: Chen from his job as a surveyor, a son from the bamboo-utensil factory where he is employed, that son's wife and another son, both farm workers, and two youngsters, a girl of 10 and a boy of 13. (There is little casual chatter during the meal; instead the family listens to a commune-sponsored broadcast of music, news and propaganda.)

Assessing the overall impact of the Communist regime, observers agree that the Chinese nuclear family is very much alive. Anthropologist Maurice Freedman reports that it has been reduced to occupying "the interstices of larger institutions—the work group, the dining hall, the nursery. . . The family has become an institution for producing babies and enjoying the leisure time left over from the major pursuits of everyday life." This description might very well apply to a nuclear family in any Western nation, particularly if both of the parents have jobs. Goode believes that even today the nuclear family remains the basic unit of Chinese society, and Bronfenbrenner goes so far as to suggest that Communist efforts to weaken the family have in fact strengthened it.

If dictatorial attempts to create a substitute for the family have had only small effect, so too has gentle persuasion. Voluntary associations of people banding together to improve the condition of the human species by devising a replacement for the family run into serious difficulties, although of a different order from those encountered when reform is attempted on a nationwide, compulsory basis. Such associations not only have to struggle against the deeply ingrained prejudices of their members and their persistent hankering after the old ways they were brought up in, but they also have to face the opposition, often the outright antagonism, of the surrounding world and, what is still more dangerous, the compelling attraction that the outside world exerts. As long as the flame of idealism burns bright, voluntary communes may survive proudly even in the face of a hostile or uncomprehending society. When idealism dies down, however, the gravitational pull of the outer world grows stronger, and they find themselves conforming more and more to the life style of the masses around them.

At thousands of places both urban and rural throughout the Western world, experimental communes have sprung up, placing themselves deliberately in opposition to the independent family. There is wide diversity in the movement, with almost as many underlying philosophies as there are communes. A few communities permit, encourage or even insist on a sexual freedom that verges on promiscuity. Others are strictly monogamous, with what is often a surprisingly puritanical attitude toward sex. What they have in common is a plan for child rearing. All of them insist on bringing up their children in a milieu wider than that of the nuclear family; instead of just a single father and mother, each child has all of the adults who live in his commune as parents.

The difficulty of eradicating old habits and ways of thought is indicated by a querulous note in the history of Twin Oaks, a commune created in 1967, and patterned in some ways after one described by Harvard behaviorist B. F. Skinner in his novel, *Walden Two*. In Twin Oaks, it is not parents but a Child Manager who lays down the law about what children are to do and what they may not do. But in real life most parents are all too prone to revert to "wicked" familial ways, and such a situation is described in Kathleen Kincade's chronicle of Twin Oaks, *A Walden Two Experiment*. A father named Pete objected violently because the women who belonged to the commune were letting his daughter Maxine run around barefoot and catch cold. "Where was the Child Manager then?" Kincade asks. "Why did he not interfere and tell Pete that the Community's children would be allowed to go barefoot inside the house? Brian, like the rest of us, was cowed by Pete. . . . As long as Maxine was with us, it was Pete who was de facto child manager."

Experiments like Twin Oaks rarely survive more than a few years. But the post-World War II communes are so young and involve such tiny numbers of people that few conclusions can be drawn from their successes or failures. There are, however, two older experiments in communal living with sizable memberships, impressive life spans, and a wide store of experience to examine: the Oneida community in upstate New York and the kibbutz movement in Israel.

Oneida was the creation of that monogamy-hating Yankee, John Humphrey Noyes. Everything at Oneida was owned or shared in common, including sex. Oneidans formed sexual relationships with one another as and when they wished, but their wishes were supposed to conform to what Noyes called the principle of "ascending fellowship," that is, the young and the inexperienced were matched with older people, often in rooms set aside for what were euphemistically called "social purposes." Noyes was appalled by what he regarded as the exclusiveness and selfishness of love between two people, and all the force of the community was mobilized in an effort to prevent such a thing from occurring. When romantic attachments developed anyway, the guilty parties generally felt ashamed of themselves, and sooner or later they confessed their sin and begged their fellow Oneidans for forgiveness.

For almost 30 years the community people lived by the Noyes principles, but the experiment lost its initial zeal, the bizarre sexual practices were abandoned in response to the increasing hostility of the society outside and Oneida turned into the pleasant and prosperous city in upper New York State that it remains today.

A more ambitious and longer-lived experiment began in the Middle East a few years after the end of the Oneida one. This was the kibbutz movement, started by idealistic Jews from Eastern Europe who expected to inaugurate a new, socialist phase of human history by founding communities based on common ownership, manual labor for all and suppression of the old family system.

At the beginning of the movement, anti-familial bias was extreme, perhaps because the founders had experienced so much stress and anguish in breaking away from their own tradition-bound families in Eastern Europe. Formal marriages were regarded as unnecessary: a boy and a girl who wanted to live together simply moved into the same room. Husbands and wives did not work or eat together, and were encouraged to spend their leisure time with the whole group rather than by themselves. To make a public display of affection was considered a serious breach of good manners. Children were given over by their mothers shortly after birth to be raised with other children of the same age by specially trained nurses called *metaplot*.

Even under this system, it was soon discovered that children and parents formed strong attachments to each other anyway. Although they were allowed only a few hours a week together, the time represented a little interlude of human warmth in all the discipline and lofty idealism of the kibbutz program. Children who were treated just like their peers by the *metaplot* could be petted and spoiled by their parents to their hearts' content in these brief encounters. Through such cracks in the stern wall of theory, life in the kibbutz began to be transformed. The wall was further breeched when the kibbutzim, poor agricultural settlements hacked out of the stony soil of Palestine 60-odd years ago, became prosperous, and frequently industrialized, communities, with all the temptations material success brings with it. Not surprisingly, many old rules softened.

Today the kibbutz remains an institution far removed from the family structure familiar in the West. Yet it is apparent that it is losing its basically nonfamilial nature. Apparently certain human needs can best be met through the family—despite all the arguments and reformist indignation of the anti-family ideologies.

The evidence of the communes proves that the family is not dead. It is not even dying. "Just as deer and buffalo are herding animals, fish are schooling animals and birds are flocking animals, human beings are family animals," anthropologist Paul Bohannan of Northwestern University asserts. "It's in our fibre, one of the behavioral dimensions of our genes."

Indestructible though the family may be, it is not unchangeable. It has thus adapted in small ways and large over the millennia, and the pressures for further evolution are stronger today than ever. For one thing, many experts predict more, rather than less, divorce in years to come. So-

continued on page 158

Oneida: one man's utopia

John Humphrey Noyes

In 1848, a preacher born in Vermont named John Humphrey Noyes, who was as doughty and determined as he looked *(left)*, incorporated a group of fervent followers into the Oneida Community in northern New York State. It proved one of the more bizarre attempts to replace the nuclear family with another living arrangement.

Noyes' disciples, convinced that they could gain spiritual perfection by submerging personal interests in the common good, gave their property to the community. Then they set about making Oneida self-supporting by manufacturing animal traps, travel bags and silverware. Oneida prospered and grew:

after one year there were 87 members; two years later membership was 205.

Not only was private property outlawed, private attachments were too. In place of monogamy, Noyes introduced "complex marriage"—every man considered himself married to every woman, and vice versa. Oneidans could form sexual relationships freely, but if love developed, the erring partners had to confess their sin and apologize to the rest of the community. The system was the most radical, though not the only, departure the Oneidans made from social practices of the day, and eventually it aroused passions that led to the failure of their bold experiment.

The Oneidans liked croquet because everybody—men, women and children—could play it together. This game took place in the 1860s.

Community women wore their hair and their skirts short—the latter over ankle-length pantaloons. The fashion freed them to work alongside the men.

For a 19th Century religious community, Oneida was surprisingly worldly. There were no formal religious services and no strictures against dancing, partying, card games or theatricals. Other diversions included everything from Greek lessons and a Turkish bath to early-day encounter groups.

Yet for all its utopian aspects, in 1880 the Oneida Community came to an end, some 30 years after it had begun. The breakup was precipitated by anger over John Noyes' sexual habits—he insisted on initiating young girls of the community into complex marriage. Noyes finally fled with a handful of loyal followers to Canada, where he ended his days in obscurity.

But without a strong leader to succeed him, the remaining members fell into hopeless bickering over the issue of complex marriage. Finally, the community was dissolved and reformed into an ordinary industrial corporation, which has since become known for the silverware it continues to manufacture in Oneida. As for the members, some married, others became celibate. The nonfamilial system that had worked for one generation had failed for that generation's children. They had returned to the family, the apparently indestructible scheme for human living.

At the top of his patriarchal power around 1860, John Noyes stands in t right foreground, his arms folde surrounded by the Oneida Communi

In the late 1850s, all hands turn out for a pea-shelling bee designed to make a tiresome chore more pleasant.

ciologist Sidney Aronson believes that "People will still get married. The difference is that they will do it more often." The trend that Aronson predicts has already been recognized in a *New Yorker* magazine cartoon depicting a young man proposing to his girl with the words, "Will you be my first wife?" Some experts think that the increase in divorce will occur in middle life, after children are grown. Others expect it to come early, before children are born to a couple. The anthropologist Margaret Mead suggests that future societies may want to authorize two quite different kinds of marriage. In the first, the avowed intention would be to refrain from having any children. This kind of marriage would be easy to dissolve, and in actual practice would very often end in divorce, with no harm done either to society or to individuals. In the second, which would require a special license and a special ceremony, the intent would be to have children, and to stay together until they were grown.

If Mead is right, average family size will continue to decrease. Many factors—economic, social, moral—could accelerate this trend. For a couple of centuries now, the world has been undergoing unparalleled expansion, both in population and in exploitation of the world's energy resources. Levels of prosperity, even in the poorest countries, have risen dramatically. Such circumstances provide an ideal, and unusual, stimulant for the formation of families; if there is an abundance of everything to go round, if there is work either on the land or in factories, people have no trouble in marrying off their children, and they in turn have no scruples about having children of their own. But in a contracting or stable economy (as even rich America discovered during the Depression of the '30s), marriage and birth rates decline abruptly because fewer people feel they can afford to start families.

There is no guarantee that world-wide economic expansion will go on indefinitely; in fact, there have been strong indications in recent years that it will not, if only because the energy that would be needed to support continued expansion may not be available. For this and other reasons, some authorities believe that the world cannot sustain many more people than it now has. This belief is the driving force behind Zero Population Growth, a movement that calls on families to restrict themselves to the number of children required to keep the population more or less stable.

Spurred by ZPG arguments, or perhaps by new government policies providing economic incentives for smaller families, or simply by personal inclination, many couples throughout the world may renounce the idea of having several children. Most of them probably will not give up parenthood, however. Although what Alex Comfort calls recreational and relational (as opposed to reproductive) sex may become increasingly important in future families, behavioral experts believe that most husbands and wives will continue to reproduce themselves. Bohannan calls parenthood a major life experience that few people will renounce, whatever the incentives, and psychiatrist Theodore Lidz adds: "I don't know whether having children is a basic genetic drive or not. But a large proportion of people have the feeling that their lives as adults become meaningful if they have a feeling of some kind of continuity into the future."

These views of the future are based on each couple's new-found ability to exert certain control over family size through improved contraceptive devices and techniques. The Pill, in particular, has given women a previously unattainable mastery of their destiny within the family. "The role of the woman is changing from female to human being; . . . in this respect, the family is growing stronger," says sociologist Philip Hauser. And this step toward sexual equality is evidenced by the growth of family support systems—child-care centers and other institutions that take some of the pressure off mothers. Day nurseries, for instance, increasingly make it possible for women to work without disrupting family life.

Increasing transfers of onetime family responsibilities to the state seem inevitable because as Otto Pollak of the University of Pennsylvania notes, there are many areas where external institutions are more efficient. A schoolteacher is better at explaining differential calculus to children than mother and dad are.

But there is much of life that cannot be captured or contained by the coarse meshes of even the most efficient bureaucracy. It is here, on the informal, human side that the family has gained. The gain is in emotional intensity. The family, now less autonomous in its relations with the outside world than it used to be in generations past, now has far more say in arranging its own inner patterns. Once designed chiefly to perform specific social tasks, it concentrates more today on satisfying individual cravings for affection and for solidarity.

The family remains a rock and a refuge from the impersonal, rational and computerized world outside. Within its protective embrace, people are not interchangeable counters to be moved around according to some impersonal reckoning. At home, family members can unbutton and be their own sloppy, un-card-catalogued selves.

The family of the future, Pollak says, "should be visualized as a place of intimacy in a world of loose and depersonalized relationships." He visualizes it as "an organization of self-help and regeneration for the battles of bureaucratic existence."

Unreconstructed patriarchs like Clarence Day, Jr., the author of *Life with Father*, or the late Joseph P. Kennedy might find this a pretty paltry, namby-pamby substitute for the family in its Victorian prime, when it cut an imposing figure in the social world and laid down the law in manners and morals to all its members. But the family in the Victorian world was only one of the myriad forms this protean institution has assumed. If Pollak is right, the world may be heading back to the original form, the one that took shape in some Pleistocene cave with a naked ape man and ape woman crooning over their frightened child while the saber-toothed cat thrashed about outside. Perhaps it was just the crying child's need for comfort that both started the family and makes it eternal.

Three generations on a kibbutz

The most durable alternative to the traditional family that has yet been devised is the Israeli kibbutz, or collective settlement, in which everyone owes loyalty not only to his individual family, but also to his community as a whole. The 60,000 or so adult Israelis on the nation's 227 collectives have yielded a large share of personal autonomy to their kibbutzim, including the privilege of choosing their own jobs and of gaining personal wealth. But more startling, many have surrendered their right to raise their own children.

On most kibbutzim, the children are raised apart from their parents. Mother and father generally live in a modest two-room apartment, while their youngsters are reared from the age of about six weeks by specially trained nurses in separate residences housing perhaps 20 children each.

The unusual features of kibbutz life have not, however, destroyed family ties. The Arnon family, seen at left enjoying a three-generation get-together, remain deeply devoted to their kibbutz —and also to each other. The family patriarch is Benjamin Arnon, who was born in Tel Aviv in 1911 and settled on kibbutz Mishmar Ha'emek (Guard of the Valley) in 1935. His wife, Hagar, fled Germany in 1938, the only member of her family to survive the Nazi holocaust, and joined kibbutz Mishmar Ha'emek, where she found "a sense of purpose and a feeling of belonging." Their three grown sons, Amatsia, Jonathan and Jephtah, have also remained faithful and hard-working kibbutzniks (slang for the members of a kibbutz). And a third generation of the Arnon family—the children of Amatsia and Jonathan—are also being raised in the kibbutz's communal way of life.

The Arnon family gathers outside the modest house occupied by family patriarch, Benjamin, and his wife, Hagar, who are in the center of the picture. Standing behind them is their unmarried son Jephtah, known as Ifty. At top left are Jonathan, holding daughter Maayan, and wife, Ada, holding daughter Ravith. Amatsia (glasses) is at lower left, his wife, Nurith, at far right. Their children are ranged between them: left to right, Carmel, Shaul and Michal.

PHOTOGRAPHED BY MARVIN NEWMAN

Kibbutz members vote at a meeting of Mishmar Ha'emek's general assembly, held in the communal dining hall.

Bearded Ifty Arnon (above, left) plays a spirited backgammon game with friends.

Community control in many realms

Every kibbutz is governed by a general assembly to which all members belong. It takes binding votes on issues, including many that in conventional societies are decided by families or individuals. The assembly even dictates what studies members may undertake. Nurith Arnon reports that when she told kibbutz members she wanted to become a social worker, "They argued that we didn't need a social worker here." Eventually, however, she got her way.

The assembly also has final say concerning what items are carried in the kibbutz "store." There money is not used since kibbutzniks receive only minuscule yearly cash allowances. But necessities are given out, and each member may choose about $60 worth of extras each year. A few other aspects of kibbutz life are also unregimented; for instance, there is plenty of time for recreation. Despite the assembly's wide-ranging power, communal life remains attractive to most kibbutzniks. Between 70 and 80 per cent of kibbutz-bred youths return to their kibbutz after their required stint of military training.

No money changes hands as Benjamin Arnon makes purchases at the kibbutz store.

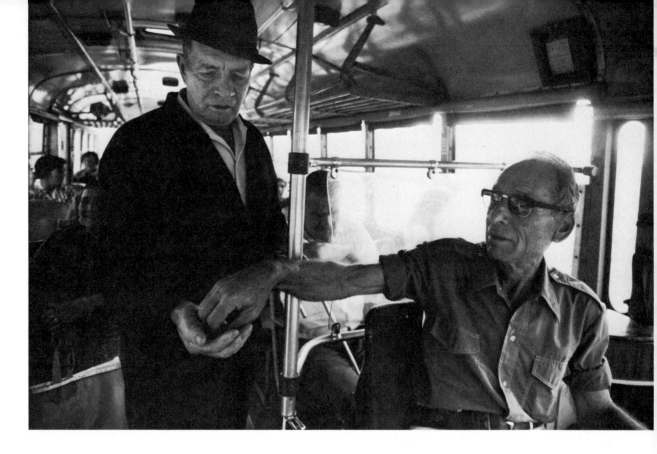

Working hard at assigned jobs

One of the few members of the kibbutz with an outside job, Benjamin Arnon makes change while driving a bus. His wages are turned over to the kibbutz.

Hard labor is the pride and purpose of every kibbutz. Jobs are assigned by the ruling body, the general assembly, to all members, including mothers since, of course, their children are cared for in the group nurseries.

The work was almost exclusively agricultural for years after the founding of the first kibbutz by immigrant Jews in 1909. Now, however, two thirds of the kibbutzim have factories producing everything from laboratory equipment to perfume, and some operate motels for tourists, who make up one of the country's major industries.

The entire Arnon family works except for the young children. Benjamin drives a bus, Hagar works in the kibbutz social club, their sons Jonathan and Amatsia both labor in Mishmar Ha'emek's plastics plant, son Ifty is a farm worker, Nurith is a high-school housekeeper, and Ada works in the dining hall. The fruit of all their labors belongs to the kibbutz, which in return clothes and feeds them.

Ada sets a table in the kibbutz's central dining hall. Working in the dining hall is considered a boring job, so members are assigned to it for only a few months.

*Ifty operates a farm machine that
stacks bales of hay. After his stint at farm
work, Ifty gained permission from
the kibbutz to take a year's travel leave.*

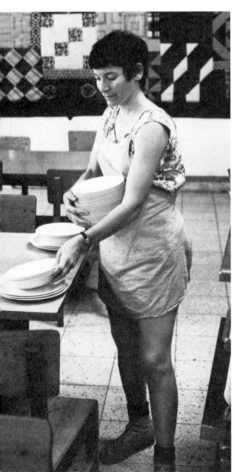

Jonathan, an engineer, repairs a machine in the plastics factory run by the kibbutz.

Four two-year-olds, including Jonathan Arnon's daughter Maayan (far left), listen as a nurse reads them a sto

For all children, group upbringing

The most controversial feature of kibbutz life is its communal method of
child rearing. Mothers are given six
weeks off from work to nurse their new
babies; then they must turn them over
to the special caretakers. However, the
mothers are granted six months of half-
time work so that they can be with their
infants the rest of the day.

But more than maternal emotions are
at stake in group upbringing. There is
debate about its impact on personality.
Many observers think the effect is noticeable: the system has produced few
major artists or musicians, but many
people suited to group endeavor. In
1972, some 25 per cent of Israel's Cab-
inet members and 40 per cent of its air
force pilots had kibbutz backgrounds
—even though the communes house
only 3 per cent of the population.

There is less agreement about the
emotional tone of the kibbutz-bred personality. Some believe it is cool and flat.
"Our children are afraid to be afraid,
afraid to love," one Israeli expert maintains—but another, psychologist Ron
Shouval, counters that kibbutz kids "are
warm underneath. It is just that the
young kibbutznik does not give up his
first layer easily."

Lunchtime in Maayan's nursery is supervised by nurses specially trained in child care.

Maayan (above, left) and friends make a social occasion of potty-sitting in their nursery home, which houses a total of 10 children.

Amatsia Arnon and son Shaul, five, enjoy a father-son outing on the kibbutz reservoir.

Family joys still undimmed

Although children live in communal nurseries, mothers and fathers see them daily, and familial love glows brightly. Between four and seven is the children's hour on Mishmar Ha'emek. The workday over, parents are free to devote themselves to their youngsters, playing with them and helping to put them to bed. They do so with joy. "On a kibbutz," says Jonathan Arnon's wife, Ada, "there are a few things we can give the children: time, love and the things we make ourselves."

This family love persists when the children are grown. The adult Arnons see one another every chance they get. On Fridays Jonathan, Ada and their children drop in on Benjamin and Hagar for coffee and cake; on Saturdays, Amatsia stops by with his wife, Nurith, and their youngsters; on other days there is much informal coming and going. Ifty and his father are frequent companions. The unusual kibbutz child-rearing arrangements, so different from the normal family, paradoxically appear not to decrease family solidarity, but rather to encourage and deepen loyalty and devotion.

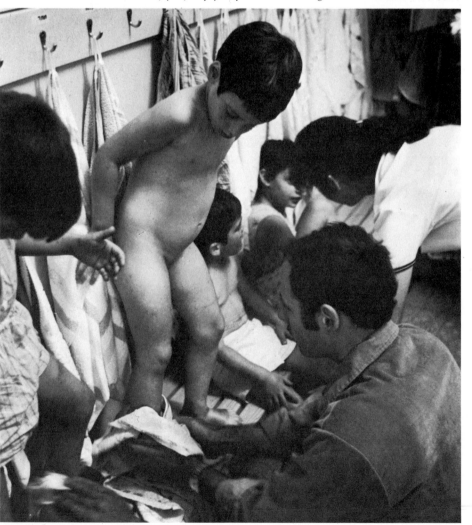

Parents, including Jonathan Arnon (foreground), ready children for bed in their nursery.

Ifty Arnon and his father, Benjamin, exchange jokes in the communal dining room.

In an informal family gathering, Ada, with her daughter Maayan on her lap, visits with Benjamin (back to camera) and Hagar.

Bibliography

*Also available in paperback.
†Available in paperback only.

†Arensberg, Conrad M., *The Irish Countryman*. Natural History Press, 1968.

*Aries, Philippe, *Centuries of Childhood*. Alfred A. Knopf, Inc., 1962.

Bell, Norman W., and Ezra F. Vogel, *A Modern Introduction to the Family*. The Free Press, 1968.

*Benedict, Ruth, *Patterns of Culture*. Houghton Mifflin Co., 1934.

*Blood, Robert O., Jr., and Donald M. Wolfe, *Husbands and Wives: The Dynamics of Married Living*. The Free Press, 1960.

*Bronfenbrenner, Urie, *Two Worlds of Childhood: U.S. and U.S.S.R.* Simon and Schuster, Inc., 1972.

*Carden, Maren Lockwood, *Oneida: Utopian Community to Modern Corporation*. Harper & Row Publishers, Inc., 1971.

Colman, Arthur D., and Libby Lee Colman, *Pregnancy: The Psychological Experience*. Herder & Herder, 1972.

Cavan, Ruth, *The American Family*. Thomas Y. Crowell Co., 1969.

*Cooper, David, *The Death of the Family*. Random House, Inc., 1971.

Curtin, Sharon, *Nobody Ever Died of Old Age*. Little, Brown & Co., 1973.

*De Beauvoir, Simone, *The Coming of Age*. G. P. Putnam's Sons, 1973.

†Fox, Robin, *Kinship and Marriage*. Penguin Books, Inc., 1967.

*Freud, Sigmund, *Totem and Taboo*. W. W. Norton & Co., Inc., 1950.

Goode, William J.:
The Family. Prentice-Hall, Inc., 1964.
Readings on the Family and Society. Prentice-Hall, Inc., 1964.
World Revolution and Family Patterns. The Free Press, 1963.

Jonsson, Gustav, *Acta Psychiatrica Scandinavica* (Supplement 195). P. Munksgaard, Copenhagen, 1967.

Kelleher, Stephen J., *Divorce and Remarriage for Catholics?* Doubleday & Co., Inc., 1973.

Kincade, Kathleen, *A Walden Two Experiment*. William Morrow & Company, Inc., 1973.

†Laing, R. D., *The Politics of Experience*. Ballantine Books, Inc., 1967.

Leslie, Gerald, *The Family in Social Context*. Oxford University Press, 1973.

*Liebow, Elliot, *Tally's Corner*. Little, Brown & Co., 1967.

*Lopreato, Joseph, *Italian Americans*. Random House, Inc., 1970.

†Mace, David and Vera, *Marriage: East and West*. Doubleday & Co., Inc., 1959.

Macoby, Eleanor E., Theodore M. Newcomb and Eugene L. Hartley, *Readings in Social Psychology*. Holt, Rinehart & Winston, Inc., 1947.

*Malinowski, Bronislaw, *The Sexual Life of Savages*. Harcourt, Brace & World, Inc., 1929.

*Mead, Margaret, *Growing Up in New Guinea*. New American Library, Inc., 1930.

Mertens, Alice, *South West Africa*. Taplinger Publishing Co., Inc., 1966.

Moore, Barrington, Jr., *Political Power and Social Theory*. Harvard University Press, 1958.

Murdock, George Peter:
Ethnographic Atlas. University of Pittsburgh Press, 1967.
†*Social Structure*. The Free Press, 1966.

Nimkoff, M. F., *Comparative Family Systems*. Houghton Mifflin Co., 1965.

Packard, Vance, *A Nation of Strangers*. David McKay Company, Inc., 1972.

Parkes, Colin, *Bereavement: Studies of Grief in Adult Life*. International Universities Press, Inc., 1973.

Reiss, I. L., *The Family System in America*. Holt, Rinehart & Winston, Inc., 1971.

Robertson, Constance Noyes, *Oneida Community: An Autobiography, 1851-1876*. Syracuse University Press, 1970.

Sennett, Richard, "The Brutality of Modern Families." *Transaction*, Sept. 1970.

Simpson, George, *People in Families/Sociology, Psychoanalysis and the American Family*. Meridian Books, 1969.

†Skinner, B. F., *Walden Two*. Macmillan Company, 1960.

*Spiro, Melford, *Kibbutz: Venture in Utopia*. Schocken Books, Inc., 1971.

†Stephens, William N., *The Family in Cross-Cultural Perspective*. Holt, Rinehart & Winston, Inc., 1963.

†Sussman, Marvin B., *Sourcebook in Marriage and the Family*. Houghton Mifflin Co., 1968.

Wolf, Bernard, *The Little Weaver of Agato*. Cowles Book Corporation, Inc., 1969.

Yang, C. K., *The Chinese Family in the Communist Revolution*. M.I.T. Press, 1959.

Acknowledgments

The authors and editors of this book wish to thank the following persons and institutions for their assistance: Norman Bell, Professor of Sociology and Psychology, University of Toronto; Paul Bohannan, Professor of Anthropology, Northwestern University, Chicago; Urie Bronfenbrenner, Professor of Human Development and Family Studies, Cornell University, New York; Jerome Bruner, Watts Professor of Psychology, Department of Experimental Psychology, Oxford University, England; John Cuber, Professor of Sociology and Anthropology, Ohio State University, and Peggy Haroff Cuber; Enid Farmer; Leny Heinen, Limburg, Germany; Elaine McCoy, Oneida Ltd. Silversmiths, Oneida, New York; Cyril C. Richards, Professor, Department of History, Union Theological Seminary, New York; Zionist Archives and Library, 515 Park Avenue, New York.

Picture Credits

Index

Numerals in italics indicate a photograph or drawing of the subject mentioned.

67; between men, 54, 55; in New Guinea, 57; of Nuer of East Africa, 54-55; between people of same sex, 54-55; in Polynesian Islands, 57; primary functions of, 54-56; of Purum of India, 60-61; rates of, 158; religious rites of, 53, 73; rules of, 53; as sacrament, 73; secondary functions of, 56-57; for social position, 67, 72; state control of, 113; stresses in, 111-127; in Sweden, 58; symbols of Christian, *61*; teen-age, 74-85, 130-131; in Trinidad, 56; in United States, 57, 62-67; for wealth, 67, 72; between women, 54-55

Marriage of Giovanni Arnolfini and Jeanne Cenami, The (painting), van Eyck, *61*

Mass media: impact of, 117, 118; as source of external ideas, 116-118

Masters, William, 144

Matchmakers, 69-72

Mate selection, 57-67; endogamy in, 62; exogamy in, 57-62; factors in, 62-67; family influence in, 67, 72; incest taboos in, 57-62; in India, 62; in Ireland, 69-72; in Japan, 69; love as basis for, 57; by matchmakers, 69-70; in Polynesian Islands, 57; restrictions on, 57-67; for social position, 67, 72; in Tasaday tribe of Mindanao, 36; for wealth, 67, 72

Mead, Margaret, 17, 57, 94, 158

Mentawei, of West Sumatra, 39

Meyer, Christel, *96-97*

Monogamous family (ies). *See* Nuclear family (ies)

Moore, Barrington, Jr., 149

Morgan, Lewis Henry, 33

Morris, Desmond, 50

Mother (s). *See* Wife (ves), role of

Mother (s) -in-law, 47, 119-120, 151

Mourning, *143*

Murdock, George Peter, 33, 60

N

Nahmias, Jesus, 126

Napoleon, 43

Nash, Ogden, 122

Navaho, 14, *15*, 134

Nayar, of India, 38-39

Niagara Falls, *68*, 69

No-fault divorce, 134

Non-familial life (ves), 149

Norway: peer group in, 115; wedding in, *65*

Noyes, John Humphrey, 149, 153, *155*, *157*

Nuclear family: of Andaman Island pygmies, 35; definition of, 21, 33; effect of adolescent subculture on, 108-109; expressive leader in, 46; in industrialized societies, 34; inheritance in, 40-42; instrumental leader in, 46; kinship in, 40-42; mixed marriages in, 42; mobility of, 34-35, 50-51; monogamous, 33, 35; religious traditions in,

42; roles of husband and wife in, 46; rules of descent in, 40-42; of Stone-age tribes, 35; of Tasaday of Mindanao, 35, 36-37. *See also* Husband (s), role of; Wife (ves), role of

Nuer, of East Africa, 54-55

Nursery (ies), state-run, *100*, 101, 152

O

Ojibways, of Canada, 133

Oneida Community, 153-154, *155-157*; "complex marriage" of, 155; John Humphrey Noyes as founder of, 149, 153, *155*, *157*; ownership of, 153; as religious community, 156; sexual freedom of, 153, 155, 156; social reaction to, 153-154

Owens, Bill, 118

P

Packard, Vance, 50

Parent (s). *See* Husband (s), role of; Wife (ves), role of

Parents Without Partners, *141*

Parkes, Colin, 142-144

Parsons, Talcott, 46, 109, 125, 130

Patrilineage, 21

Payment (s), marriage: arranged by matchmakers, 69-72; brideprice as, 68-69; bridewealth as, 68-69; of Cheyenne Indians, 68; of Chukchee of Siberia, 68; dowry as, 69; forms of, 68; of Ifugao of Philippines, 68; of Jacob in Bible, 68; of Manus of Admiralty Islands, 68; of Siane of New Guinea, 68; of Subanum of Philippines, 68; of Tiv of Nigeria, 68

Peer group, 113-116, *117*; authority of, 115; conflict of with family, 113-116, 117; functions of, 113-116

Person-centered family, 101

Plato, 147

Political function (s), of family, 11, 34

Pollak, Otto, 159

Polyandry, 35, 38-39. *See also* polygamous family (ies)

Polygamous family (ies), 33, 35-39, *41*; back street families as, 35; of Baganda of Central Africa, 38; coexistence of with nuclear family, 35; definition of, 33; demographic factors in, 38, 41; effect of industrialization on, 35; of Kikuyu of East Africa, 38; of Lango of East Africa, 35-38; of Mormons, *41*; of Nayar of India, 38-39; polyandry, 35, 38-39; polygyny, 35-38; reasons for, 35-38, 39; serial, 35; of Ukuanjama tribe, *41*

Polygyny, 35-38. *See also* Polygamous family (ies)

Polynesian Islands, 57

Potlatch, 53

Poverty, 19, 94, 102, 131

Powdermaker, Hortense, 123

Primogeniture, 42-43

Prohibition, in socializing children, 20

Pukapukas, of Polynesia, 133

Punishment, in socializing children, 17, 20, 21

Purum, of India, 60-61

R

Rajput, of India, 93

Rational Psychology, Society for, Munich, 117-118

Reiss, Ira, 38, 99

Religious function (s), of family, 11, 149

Republic, The, Plato, 147-148

Residence, rules of, 34

Responsibilities, within family, 34, 38, 40

Retarded children, 13, 87, 89, 150

Reward, in socializing children, 17, 20

Rich, Richard, descendents of, *44-45*

Rights, transfer of, 42-43

Runaways, 8

Russia: Bolshevik communes of, 150; individual in, 20; wedding ceremony in, 63

S

Sacrament, marriage as, 73

Schenkein, Allan, 89

School (s): as cause of stress, 111-112, 113; efficiency of, 159; free public, 107; state control of, 107, 113

Senility, 88

Separation, 129, 134-135

Sexual Life of Savages, The, Malinowski, 54

Sexual relationship (s), 12, 113; changes in, 8, 159; in communes, 150, 153-154, 155, 156; need for, 35-38, 144; unhappiness in, 123

Shilluk, 60

Shivaree, 53

Shouval, Ron, 166

Shtetl (s), 44-45

Shuswap, of British Columbia, 144

Siane, of New Guinea, 68

Siegle, Else, 98

Sioux Indians, 20

Skills, training in: by Americans, 17; cultural variations in, 16-17; by Eskimos, 16-17; family variations in, 16-17; by Japanese peasants, 16-17; by Manus of New Guinea, 17; by Norwegians, 17; as part of socialization, *15*, 16-17; of reading, 17; in Western nations, 17, 107. *See also* Socialization

Skinner, B. F., 153

Smirchich, R. J., 62

Social behavior, patterns of: class distinctions in, 19; cultural differences in, 19, 20; as element of socialization, 13-16, 17; family differences in, 16, 17, 20; of social position, 17-19; of status, 17-19; training in, 13-16, 17-19. *See also* Socialization

Social Security, 95-98

Socialization of children, 12-21; American, 17,

19, 20, 21; of American Indians, 19-20, 20-21; by communes, 149, 150; in Communist China, 21, 151-152; elements of, 13-16, 17; of Eskimos, 16-17; by example, *14-15*, 20-21, 142; goals of, 20, 21; importance of, 12-13, 20; of Japanese peasants, 16-17; knowledge as element of, 13-16, 17-20; of Manus of New Guinea, 17; methods of, 20-21; Norwegian, 17; in preliterate societies, 16; reading as aspect of, 17; in Russia, 21, 150; by technological societies, 16, 149, 150; variations in, 16-17, 20; in Western nations, 17
Sophocles, 93, 111
Sororate, 144
Soviet Union, women's role in, 8, 45
Spock, Benjamin, 99, 101
Spousal support, 139
State: as cause of stress, 111-112, 113; control of schools by, 113; efficiency of, 159; in establishment of communes, 149
Stem family(ies), 39
Stephens, Simon, 127
Stephens, William N., 102, 139
Stress(es), 111-127; adultery as cause of, 123-125; from aged dependents, 98-99; from disappointment of marriage partners, 122-123; divisive effect of, 127; and double standard, 123-125; eliminating sources of, *82-83*; in families with older dependent children, 107-109; from within family, 88-89, 98-101, 107-109, 111-112, *118-122*; family therapy as help for, 127; fragmentation as result of, 126; of generation gap, 107-109, *122*; from governmental institutions, 111, 112, 113; of illness, 119, *124*, 125-127; incompatibility as source of, 122; from in-laws, 47, *119*-120; in interfaith marriages, 121; in interracial marriages, 121; of marriage partners' adjustments, 119; from mass media, 116-117, 118-119, 127; from outside sources, 111-119, 133; of parenthood, 99-101, 107-109, *118, 120-122*, 131; from peer groups, 113-115, 117; of personal disasters, 119; from poverty, *114*, 115, 131; of predivorce period, 140; and relationship of marriage partners, 120-125; from relatives, 119-120; from religious institutions, 111, 112-113; retarded child as cause of, 89; from schools, 112, 113; sexual unhappiness and, 123; sources of, 82, 111-112, 115, *118-122*, 129; from threats to family authority, 111-112, 113; women's liberation movement and, 123
Subanum, of Philippines, 68
Subculture, adolescent. *See* Adolescent subculture
Suicide, 47, 142
Sullivan, Annie, 13
Symbolism, in marriage rites, 53, *61, 66*

T

Tasaday tribe, of Mindanao, *36-37*; communal living of, 36; division of responsibilities by, 36; nuclear families of, 36, *37*; as Stone-age type of people, 35, 36
Teen-age marriage(s), *74-85*, 130-131
Television: as "baby sitter," *126*, 127; impact of, 117; long-term effect of, 118; as pacifier, 117-118; as source of stress, 116, 117, 127; statistics of ownership of, 117
Thonga, of Africa, 60
Till, Emmett, 19
Titles, inheritance of, 34
Tiv, of Nigeria, 68
Trinidad, common-law marriage of, 56
Trobrianders, of southwest Pacific: adolescent society of, 109; incest rules of, 60; Malinowski's study of, 54, 109; marriage customs of, 54; as Stone-age culture, 54
Tupinamba, 60
Twin Oaks, 153

U

Ukuanjama tribe, 41
Unitarian Church, family experiment of, *151*

V

Values: of American Indians, 19-20; attitudes as, 19; class convictions as, 19; cultural differences in, 19, 20; dependence of status rules on, 19; as element of socialization, 13-16; of family, 13-16, 19, 20; of Russians, 20; and school habits, 19; training in, 13-16, 19-20. *See also* Socialization
Videotape, 127

W

Walumba, of North Australia, 40
Wedding(s), *52, 58-59, 63-66, 74-75, 76*; of Bugti of Pakistan, 63; ceremonies of, 53, *63-66*, 72-73; expenses of, 53, 73; Hindu, *65*; of Hopi Indians of U.S. Southwest, 63; in India, 63, *66*; Japanese, *64*; of Kwakiutl Indians of America, 53; of Malays of Singapore, 63; modern American, 53-54; modern European, 53; Muslim, *64*; in Ninth Century, 73; in Norway, 65; origin of word, 67, 68; potlatches as, 53; of Puritans, 73; religious rites of, 53, 73; of royalty, 63; Russian, 63; traditions in, 53-54, 73; Turkish, *64*; as universal custom, 53, 63; in Zambia, 65
Weiss, Robert, 136
White House Conference on Aging, 1971, 98
Widowed spouse(s), *138*, 139, 142-145; among Agutainos of Polowan, 144; among ancient Jews, 144; chances of remarriage of, 144; change of role of, 142-144; denial by, 142-143; depression of, 142, 143; economic predicament of, 139; emotional ties of to

dead spouse, 144-145; emotional troubles of 142; mortality rate of, 142; needs of, 144; physical illnesses of, 142; in preliterate societies, 144; pressures to remarry, 144; recovery of, 142, 143-144; remarriage customs for, 144; among Shuswap of British Columbia, 144; suicide rate among, 142; superstitions about, 144
Wife(ves), role of, 43-47, 51, 78; abortion laws and, 46-47; adultery in, 43, 123; in African villages, 8; in American cities, 8; in ancient Chinese family, 47; in Asian villages, 8; in Baganda tribe of Central Africa, 38; biological basis for, 45, 46; birth control and, 46-47; capacity of for bearing stress, 120; childbearing as, 45; in Communist China, 47; in decision-making, 45; as divorcée, 135-136; in English common law, 43; of English 17th Century yeoman's wife, 45; of Eskimo woman, 45; in European cities, 8; as expressive leader, 46; as homemaker, 78, *80-81*; and illness, 125; in Kikuyu culture of East Africa, 38; in Korea, 46; in Lango tribe of East Africa, 35-38; as mediator of child-father relationship, 46; in modern suburbia, 46; Napoleon's statement on, 43; in Nayar culture of Malabar Coast of India, 38-39; as new mother, 99-101; in orthodox Jewish *shtetls* of Eastern Europe, 44-45; as parent, 12, 80, *81*, 82, *83*, 99-101; in polygamous societies, 35-38; as purchase, 43; rules of conduct for, 43, 123; in Soviet Union, 8; and stress, 122-123; subordinate, 122-123; as surviving spouse, 142-145; in Tasaday tribe of Mindanao, 36, 37; in technological age, 8, 34, 51; traditional Japanese, 46; in United States, 8, 45; in Western world, 45; widowed, 142-145; and women's liberation movement, 123; as workers, 8
Williamson, Robert, 99
Wilson, Betty, 145
Winch, Robert, 108
Wogeo, Melanesian, 133-134
Wolf children, 12
Women, status of, 8, 34, 135, 150, 151, 152
Women's liberation movement, 123, 139
Wulamba, of North Australia, 7

Y

Yakuts, of Siberia, 90
Yeoman's wife, duties of, 45
Yi family, of Korea, 57
Youth subculture. *See* Adolescent subculture

Z

Zaibatsu, of Japan, 42
Zambia, wedding in, *65*
Zelnik, Melvin, 8
Zero Population Growth, 158

x Printed in U.S.A.